THE SPIRAL OF TIME SERIES

RAV DOVBER PINSON

THE MONTH of ELUL

vol **6**

DAYS OF INTROSPECTION
◆ AND TRANSFORMATION ◆

IYYUN PUBLISHING

Published by IYYUN Publishing
232 Bergen Street
Brooklyn, NY 11217

http:/www.iyyun.com

Iyyun Publishing books may be purchased for educational, business or sales promotional use. For information please contact: contact@IYYUN.com

Editor: Reb Matisyahu Brown

Developmental Editor: Reb Eden Pearlstein

Proofreading / Editing: Simcha Finkelstein

Cover and book design: RP Design and Development

Cover image: by Federico Parolo
© 2015 Deuteronomy Press, used with publisher's permission as a gift to the Iyyun Center. See www.circlecalendar.com for more information.

pb ISBN 978-1-7338130-2-0

Pinson, DovBer 1971-
The Month of Elul: Days of Introspection and Transformation
1.Judaism 2. Jewish Spirituality 3. General Spirituality

vol **6**

THE MONTH *of* ELUL

DAYS OF INTROSPECTION AND TRANSFORMATION

IYYUN PUBLISHING

ב"ה

THE MONTH OF ELUL

DEDICATED BY

משפחת יחיאל

למען ילדיהם

ניקה נעמי בת עדי לאה ואבי
שתחי'

ודוד בן עדי לאה ואבי
שיחי'

וזכות התורה חק' וסיועם תגן עליהם
ויזכו למלוא הפנינים נחת מילדחם
מתוך בריאות ושמחה
ויצליחו מאד בכל עסקיחם
וימלא ח' כל משאלות לבם לטובה
מתוך אושר ועושר כל הימים

חון ועושר בביתו וצדקתו עומדת לעד

CONTENTS

ॐ

OPENING

*E*ACH MONTH OF THE YEAR RADIATES WITH A DISTINCT quality and provides unique opportunities for personal growth and spiritual illumination. Accordingly, each month has a slightly different climate and represents a particular stage in the "story of the year" as expressed through the annual cycles of nature. The winter months call for practices and pursuits that are different than those of the summer months. Some months are filled with holidays and some have only one or none at all. Each month therefore has its own natural and spiritual signature.

According to the deeper levels of the Torah, each month's distinct qualities, opportunities and natural phenomena correspond to a certain set of coordinates arranged within a 12-part symbolic structure. That is, the spiritual nature of each month is articulated according to its unique entries for each of the 12 categories: 1) a permutation of G-d's Four-Letter name 2) a verse from the Torah 3) a letter of the Aleph Beis 4) the name of the month itself 5) an experiential "sense" 6) a Zodiac sign 7) a tribe of Israel 8) a body part 9) an element 10) a unit of successive Torah portions that are read during the month 11) a season of the year 12) the holidays that occur during the month.

By reflecting on these twelve themes and categories, one reveals an ever-ascending spiral of insight, understanding, and practical action. Learning to navigate and harness the nature of change by consciously engaging with the cycles of time, adds a deeper sense of purpose and heightened presence to our lives.

The present volume will delve into the spiritual nature of the month of Elul according to these 12 categories.

☾

NOTE: *For a more comprehensive treatment of this twelve-part system and the over-arching dynamics of the "story of the year," an in-depth introduction has been provided in Volume One of this series, The Spiral of Time: Unraveling the Yearly Cycle..*

Overview
Elul: Days of Introspection & Transformation

*C*ALENDARS ARE SCRIPTS. THEY PROVIDE THE STORYLINE AND stage directions for the year based on movements of the earth in relation to other celestial bodies. In the story of terrestrial time, which all calendars strive to tell, there is most often one other primary protagonist in relation to the earth, this being either the sun or the moon. Throughout the world, virtually every calendar tells the story of the earth's correspondence with one of these two celestial characters as they chart their path across the sky. Every calendar, that is, except for the Hebrew calendar. In our calendar, there are two simultaneous and interlocking stories functioning within the year; we collate and count time by both the solar and lunar cycles.

From the lunar cycle we count the months of the year. From the solar cycle, we count the days of the year. Thus, there are two different calendrical 'new years;' the lunar cycle begins with the first *month* of the year, Nisan, while the solar cycle begins with the first *day* of the year, Rosh Hashanah. The days of Elul are therefore the final 29 days of the yearly cycle determined by the sun. According to the lunar count of months, however, Elul is the sixth month.

The names of the months that we have today were imported from the Babylonian Exile upon our return to Israel (*Yerushalmi*, Rosh Hashanah, 1:2. *Medrash Rabbah*, Bereishis, 48:9. *Tosefos*, Rosh Hashanah, 7a. *Ramban*, Shemos, 12:2). Before the Babylonian Exile, as we have explored in other volumes, the names of the months were known by their sequence within the year. For example, the Torah calls the month of Av "the Fifth Month," and Iyyar "the Second Month." There are some months, however, that *did* have a unique name — Nisan, for example, was called *Chodesh haAviv* / Month of the Spring (*Shemos*, 13:4. 23:15). Elul is another such month: the Torah calls Elul the אחרית שנה / *Acharis Shanah* / end of the year (*Devarim*, 11:12. *Rosh Hashanah*, 8a).

This concept of an *Acharis* / end is valuable to explore. For example, ending projects can often seem harder for us than beginning projects. When people begin a project there is likely a lot of enthusiasm and excitement with the sense of newness. Once the project is nearing completion and it is time to tie up the final details, that sense of newness may no longer be present. At this point in the process, many people tend to feel overly-burdened and desire to move on to their next new project.

It is much easier to cook a meal then to wash the dishes and clean up. New projects, jobs, academic terms, and personal relationships bring feelings of exhilaration and hope in their potential. A new resolution to study Torah is always carried out the next day, but the drive and commitment may start to fade a week later.

When Rebbe Leibele Eiger, the grandson of the famous scholar Rabbi Akiva Eiger, became a *Chasid* / follower of Rebbe Mendel of Kotzk it caused turmoil in his family. A respected Rabbinic scion of a non-Chasidic lineage traveling to submit himself to a Chasidic Rebbe was sometimes seen as a family 'tragedy.' In fact, some of his family even sat Shiva for Reb Leibele, as if he had died. When he came home for the first time after becoming a Chasid, his father asked him, "Was all the distress you caused worth it? What, if anything, have you learned in Kotzk?" Reb Leibele answered respectfully: "Three things have I learned: One, there is man and there are angels. Two, if man truly desires he can rise above angels. Three, *Bereishis Bara Elokim* means 'G-d creates beginnings,' but it is man who creates endings."

Starting things is easy. Inspiration strikes, adventure calls, novelty and new possibilities excite and motivate us. This is what it means that 'Hashem creates beginnings'; they are gifts from beyond. But 'we create endings.' The finish line is where we reveal our true potential. Completing a new project, seeing a dream through to its tangible manifestation, this is up to us. Cleaning up our creative mess, not making it, is where we see what we are really made of.

"There is no resoluteness like a person who has just begun a new spiritual path" (*Rokeach*. See *Pri Tzadik,* Beshalach). We all start strong, but we cannot realistically take credit for that strength, because "Hashem creates beginnings." Beginnings are a gift from Above, as are the accompanying feelings of inspiration and passion. We *can* however take credit for how we '*end*' ["Mitzvos are called after one who completes them" *Sotah*, 13b. *Tanchumah*, Ekev, 6]. Elul is thus about good endings, and finishing our work with consciousness, diligence, strength and patience.

It is, as we learn, also true that "beginnings are difficult" (*Mechilta, Rashi*, Shemos, 19:5), but the inspiration, hope, and vision that we receive from Above as we set out on a new path gives us the ability to overcome that difficulty. Endings, on the other hand, are entirely up to us. There is no analogue for "beginner's luck," when it comes to completing a task or project.

You may ask, why is completing things so difficult? One reason may be, if at the conclusion of a cycle or process, we already have our eye on the beginning of something else, our focus will be dispersed. We thus become jealous of another future moment, and as a result, we lose the passion and strength needed for full engagement in the present moment.

Elul thus contains a paradox. On the one hand, we are tasked with finishing the old year, while at the same time, there is a palpable excitement stirring inside us for the new year. As a general principle we need to be careful to stay present as we encounter endings in our life; when we are able to end the year with strength and focus, we can start the next year with greater momentum and awareness.

As we mentioned, Elul is called the *Achris Shanah* / end of the year. This term is derived from the following Torah verse, referring to the Land of Israel: "The eyes of Hashem your G-d are always upon it, from the beginning of השנה /*haShanah* / the year to the end of שנה /*Shanah* / year" (*Devarim*, 11:12). The 'beginning of the year' is Rosh haShanah (*Rosh haShanah*, 8a), the 'end of the year' is Elul. In the Hebrew there is a nuance that is lost in translation: the beginning of the year is called *haShanah* / *the* year, and the end of the year is simply called *Shanah* / year. When the new year arrives, we all say, "This year is going to be *the* year. This is the year that I will learn more Torah, the year I will begin to pray more deeply, the year I will begin to be a better husband or wife, son or daughter. This is the year I will begin to eat more healthily…." Some of us even keep these resolutions for a period of time. But sadly, as the year comes to a close, we are likely to look back and say, "Well, that was just '*a* year.' It did not turn out to be *the* year. But next year will for sure be *the* year."

If we really want to grow and really want this year to be '*the* year' we need to ensure that we end strong in Elul. We don't want to give up steam and say, "Oh well, I only have 30 days left to this year, so let me just move on and start thinking about what comes next." We need to be able to tie the end of the past year into the beginning of the coming year. In order to do this, we need to stay present with where we are at; we must contemplate the year that is almost complete, and own it. In this way, we will continue to add positive value to the past year before it is over, so we finish it well. Then we can move on to the next year from a place of clarity and groundedness.

"Ezra enacted a decree for the Jewish people that they should read the portion of the curses... that are recorded in the book of Devarim before Rosh Hashanah.* What is the reason? כדי שתכלה השנה וקללותיה / In order that the year may conclude together with its curses" (*Megilah*, 31b). But what does the year and 'its curses' mean? Does every year really have its own particular curses? Perhaps this is an allusion to the struggle people have with endings — the 'curse' being the end of the year itself. From this perspective, every end is a type of 'curse' or hardship (which is really an opportunity), something that we need to overcome and transform into 'blessing' before we start a new year.

In short, if we do not end the year consciously, we will not be able to move forward properly. When we do not own our past before letting it go, it will resurface and continue to repeat itself.

The Zohar teaches, "When a person passes on, their soul is forbidden to leave the body, and it is unable to be in the presence of the Creator or to enter a new body, until its previous body has been buried. The soul is thus unable to re-emerge and become another life-form until its former body is interred" (*Zohar* 3, p. 88a). This suggests that one's past experiences are not to be ignored and left unburied, so to speak. We need to deal with them so that we can

---

* The Rambam says, "The common custom throughout all Israel is to complete the [reading of] the Torah in one year. There are those who finish the Torah reading in a three-year cycle, however this is not a widely accepted custom." *Hilchos Tefilah,* 13:1. Today, the reading of the curses in Devarim is part of the yearly cycle, and occurs a short time before Rosh Hashanah. Perhaps, even within the custom of reading the entire Torah over the course of three years (*Megilah*, 29b), there was a special reading of the curses on the Shabbos before Rosh Hashanah. *Pri Tzadik*, Ki Savo.

move on. Every experience, no matter how negative, must be 'put to rest' before we can move on with life in a conscious manner.

Ending the year on a positive note, with cultivated authenticity and compassionate awareness, allows us to make a strong beginning, (founded on the strength of Elul, as the word Elul comes from the root word E'l (*Imrei Emes*, Ki Savo) that means strength. *Shulchan Aruch*, Orach Chayim, 5), with a real sense of *Hischadshus* / renewal. It takes intelligence to know when and how to start something, but it takes even greater intelligence to know when and how to end. Elul is all about such endings, and learning how to consciously complete things.

One way to think about this is that in Elul we inhale our past year, take it in, and assume full responsibility for the way we lived our past year. When we do the appropriate *Teshuvah* / returning to our highest truth, we can gently say goodbye to the past. Then we can freely exhale our energies into the open field of the future year.

The truth is, the way we end something reveals the true relationship we had with it all along. When a person completes a session of Torah study, for example, the manner in which he kisses the book, or the way he affectionately puts it away, shows his love for the content of his learning. Similarly, when the year is coming to a close the way we 'kiss' and 'put away' our past experiences reveals how much we honor and have learned from them.

It is recorded in the Gemara that the great sage Rabbi Akiva once admonished his son, "You should not enter into your home suddenly, without warning — how much more so into the home of a friend" (*Pesachim*, 112a). Just as there is an art or sensitivity to how one enters a home, there is an art to how one leaves it. However, some people are better at entering than exiting with grace. For example, it may be common to be skilled in making good first impressions at a new job and beginning to work with responsibility and positive energy. It is perhaps more rare to be skilled in completing and leaving a job with the same kind of responsibility and positive energy.

When endings come along many people become tired, impatient and irritable. The weight of unrectified or unprocessed thoughts, words, and deeds may seem too heavy to address. The seductive promise of new lightness and gratification pulls them out of a relationship with the responsibilities of the present. Only Teshuvah gives us the strength to gather and patiently hold the past in redemptive remembrance as we stand on the threshold of the new. Only turning towards our Source allows us to bid the past goodbye and to release it in such a way that we can move into a higher level of living now, this new year.

Rosh Hashanah is called 'the birthday of the world.' The *Shefa* / flow that created and re-creates our world on that day is like a Divine 'exhale.' As Hashem exhales and breathes new life into the world on Rosh Hashanah, we too exhale and blow the Shofar. In the period preceding Rosh Hashanah however, both humanity and Divinity draw a deep 'inhale' in order to exhale more powerfully on Rosh Hashanah. This inhale is the month of Elul. In this way, the movement from Elul to Tishrei, from the end of one year to the beginning of the next, can be seen as a cosmic breathing practice, as we reflect upon and renew our lives in concert with our Creator.

Similar to the human exhale, the Divine 'exhale' can be articulated into speech. Divine speech too is made up of 'letters' — spiritual 'sounds' or metaphysical vibrations, which give rise to physical vibrations or energies, which in turn congeal into matter. The first stage of Divine speech is the 'H' sound of the letter Hei, a subtle wind in the 'Mouth' of the Creator, so-to-speak. The other letters of Divine speech are formed when this 'wind' passes through the Five *Gevuros*, the five types of spiritual 'constriction.' These five constrictions correspond to the five areas of the mouth through which Hebrew consonants are articulated (the throat, palate, tongue, teeth and lips). By constricting the flow of the exhale, these five kinds of 'consonants' create differentiated vibrations such as *Yehi Ohr* / Let there be light. Light then comes into being through the consonants that spell the word *Ohr*. Likewise, a stone (in Hebrew, *Ehven*) is a material expression of the spiritual vibrations of the letters Aleph-Beis-Nun, which spell *Ehven*.

Words thus create reality. And before we use our words, both from the liturgy as well as our own personal prayers, to re-create our own reality on Rosh Hashanah, we must prepare ourselves. Spiritually speaking, we must draw a deep 'inhale' before we speak. We therefore 'inhale' the entire past year, turn inward, and gather our life into awareness. We can then own our past choices and challenges, by acknowledging and taking account of them. Elul is thus dedicated to Teshuvah and soul-searching.* The practice of soul-searching and ownership of our past helps us return to our

---

* *Tur*, Orach Chayim, 581; *Beis Yoseph* and the *Bach* ad loc.; *Me'am Lo'ez*, Devarim, Netzavim, 30:11-14. According to the Beis Yoseph's interpretation of the Tur, this idea of doing Teshuvah in Elul is illustrated in the Medrash *Pirkei deRebbe Eliezer*, 46. See also: *Menoras haMaor*, Ner 5. Klal 2:1, 1:2. Having undergone the long process of Teshuvah during Elul, the slate is completely cleansed when Rosh Hashanah arrives. *Reishis Chochmah*, Sha'ar haTeshuvah, 4. See also *Ohev Yisroel*, Parshas Re'eh.

inner innocence and to re-imagine what our lives could be. Then, from this place of honesty and hope, we are prepared to turn outward and recreate ourselves; we are ready to exhale and speak our world into being.

In order for Creation to remain in existence there must be a continuous alternation of inhale and exhale, life-energy running or withdrawing into transcendence, and then returning to the world anew.

The thirty days of Elul correspond to the thirty days that the "captive woman" mentioned in Parshas Ki Tetze (*Zohar Chadash*, Ki Tetze, 58b) is encouraged to weep and mourn for her lost family and culture (*Devarim*, 21:13): "And she shall weep for her father and mother for *Yerech* / a moon or thirty days" (*Yevamos*, 48b).* This time of weeping is part of the captive woman's process of coming to terms with the end of her previous life and preparing for her new life. Every movement in life, even for the better, is laced with sadness, as the old paradigm is ending. When we want to move forward and grow in the coming year, we need to take the time to properly mourn or feel remorse for our past. Only then can we release and open ourselves to the new 'exhale,' and the new life that Hashem is waiting to give us.

Elul is in this sense a real process of 'ending,' and even mourning our past year. On the other hand, this month also has the element of 'beginning' within it. In fact, Rosh Chodesh Elul itself is called a 'Rosh Hashanah' (Mishnah, *Rosh Hashanah*, 1:1). In the Northern

---

* Our sages use this verse as a support for the laws stipulating that one should mourn for a deceased relative for a period of 30 days. Rambam, *Hilchos Avel*, 6:1.

Hemisphere Elul usually corresponds to the end of the summer and the beginning of the school year. One often has significant expectations for themselves and for others connected to this new season and cycle.

Before or during Elul many people are returning from their summer vacations, where they have been indulging and enjoying themselves during the warmer months. They are most likely well-rested and filled with grandiose dreams of the coming year. Along with their sense of satiation, they may also feel self-important or 'full of themselves,' perhaps with a bit of inflated ego following such a period of relaxation and frivolity. On the other hand, people who are filled with a sense of dread when thinking of the fast-approaching coming year — or who with despondency or even boredom say to themselves, 'Oy vey, another year' — are likewise expressing a sense of misaligned ego. Whether we are faced with ego inflation or ego deflation, we are presented with a clear task in Elul: to develop a balanced sense of *Kavod* / honor and self-respect, knowing before Whom we are living our life, and taking our potential and purpose seriously.

☾

ﭏﭏ

PERMUTATION OF HASHEM'S NAME

*T*HE FOUR LETTER ESSENTIAL NAME, YUD-HEI-VAV-HEI (Hashem), is the Divine Source of all Reality. The last three letters of the Name, Hei-Vav-Hei, create the word *Hoveh* / is. The root of this verb means 'to bring into being.' The first letter of the Name, Yud, serves as a prefix to the last three letters: *Yud-HoVeH*. In this way, the Yud modifies the verb to represent a perpetual activity (see *Iyov*, 1:5). The Divine Name can thus be understood to mean, 'That Which is Continuously Bringing Being into Being.'

For numerous reasons, the Essential Name cannot be spoken. Therefore a common practice is to rearrange its four letters into an alternate construction that may be pronounced as HaVaYaH, which literally means 'Being-ness.' This aspect of the Name refers to the Ultimate Being, which is the Source and Substance of all that is. The Ultimate Being does not depend on anything else to exist. It gives rise to all past, present and future manifestations, thereby bringing all things into existence ex nihilo, i.e., *Yesh meAyin* / something from nothing. Accordingly, the individual words for was / *Havah*, is / *Hoveh*, and will be / *Yihyeh*, are all encoded within the Essential Name Itself.

Hashem, the Essential Four-Letter Name, is the Source of all being and time, and is thus *connected* to actual time. On account of this inherent connection, each unique period in time is imbued with a special expression of the Essential Name. In terms of the months, this energy is expressed through a unique permutation of the four letters that comprise the Essential Name. Therefore, each month has an inner light that 'shines' through the 'prism' of a different permutation of the four letters of the Divine Name. Each permutation communicates a different spiritual dynamic which is part of the Divine signature encoded within that particular month.

The sequence of the four letters in Hashem's 'name' which corresponds to the month of Elul is *Hei–Hei–Vav–Yud.*

---

* The vowels in the sequence of Hashem's name for the month of Elul are Kubutz-Hei, Chirik-Hei, Kamtaz-Vav, and Chirik-Yud. Although this letter-sequence is derived from the final letters of the Verse of the Month below, we use the *nekudos* or vowels from the first letters in that verse.

In the view of our Sages, a 'lower' entity receives from a 'higher' entity; 'receptive' entities are envisioned as being below 'giving' entities. Of the four letters in Hashem's name, two are considered *Mekabel* / receptive letters (Hei and Hei), and two are considered *Mashpia* / giving letters (Vav and Yud). The letter sequence of Elul thus flows from below to above; first there is the lower *Mekabel* (the lower Hei), then the upper *Mekabel* (the upper Hei), then the lower *Mashpia* (the Vav), and finally the higher *Mashpia* (the Yud).

This sequence graphically describes the process of *Teshuvah* / spiritually returning the lives we have received to the supernal Giver of Life. In fact, the word *Teshuvah* is spelled the same as the phrase *Tashuv-Hei* / returning the Hei (*Zohar* 3, 122a). During Elul, as we work on returning our lives into conscious alignment with our Creator, we follow the path of movement from 'below to above,' elevating ourselves towards the higher Mashpia. To end the year well, we must draw in our entire past year and do *Teshuvah* or *Tashuv-Hei*, returning it all to its supernal Source. Only then can we move forward in the coming year with clarity, conviction and compassion.

The lower Hei of Hashem's name symbolizes our actions, while the upper Hei symbolizes our mindset. The first stage of 'returning the Hei' thus involves rectifying our actions. However, if we merely (or robotically) replace destructive actions with constructive ones, there still may be no internal change within our overall mindset, our actions may thus later revert back to their unrectified state. How do we then change our mindset, our deeper self, to the extent that we instinctively and automatically act in positive, healthy ways? In other words, how do we consciously nurture a new 'second nature'?

For starters, it is important to point out that not only can you not change your mindset through actions alone, you also cannot change your mindset by changing your 'mind' alone. This is because the ego that inhabits the mind is designed to protect itself. Reasoning with yourself that you must change your mindset for such and such a reason, no matter how convincing, engages this self-protective ego even more. To change your mindset, you must reach beyond your mind. You must 'trick' the egoic element in your mind and go deeper.

One way to leapfrog your egoic mind is to perform repetitive small positive actions until a new positive pattern becomes deeply lodged in the psyche and manifests as your new modus operandi. This newly established second nature becomes your new reactive self or positively-inclined default setting. In other words, to effectively reset a pattern of behavior you need to take small action-based baby steps. If you find yourself doing reactive or negative actions over and over again, you can reprogram your subconscious mind by doing small proactive deeds over and over again.

Rebbe Mendel of Rimanov teaches in the name of the Arizal (*Ilana d'Chaya*, Ohr haNer, Os 40. See also *Tzetel Katan*, 16), that to undo negative patterns of behavior a person should refrain from them for 40 days, corresponding to the 40 days of *Yetziras haVelad* / formation of a child in the womb. After this period it is possible that a new nature will be created. Put more simply, to break a pattern, try to hold off for at least forty days, after that it will become easier, as this new pattern set in your nature will offset the previous one. For instance, let's say you have a reactive behavior that when you hear someone's name mentioned you chime in with a little gossip about that person. For the next forty days, every time you are drawn to say a little gossip, respond by holding your tongue for 60 seconds. Over time, beyond the forty days, the 'muscles' for refraining from gossip will become stronger and stronger.

This time period of 40 days corresponds to the time of Elul, the *Yetziras haVelad* of the creation of the world. Indeed, the 30 days of Elul and the first 10 days of Tishrei culminating in Yom Kippur are exactly 40 days. This period dedicated to Teshuvah is thus the most appropriate time to reset negative patterns of behavior. This action-based Teshuvah is on the level of the lower Hei of Hashem's name.

Another, complementary way to transform ourselves is to directly influence the inner recesses of the mind through creative visualization and imagery. This is Teshuvah on the level of the higher Hei. Both of these methods, changing action and changing consciousness through rectified imagination, reach a part of us that is beyond the surface mechanical levels of body or mind. Later, in this book, we will discuss these strategies of transformation in greater detail.

ᴙ
TORAH VERSE

*T*he four letter Divine name that shines during each month is rooted within a particular verse in the Torah (*Tikunei Zohar,* Hakdamah 9b. *Eitz Chayim,* Sha'ar 44:7). There is thus is a special verse for each month comprised of a four-word sequence, in which each word either begins or ends with one of the four letters in the Divine Name, arranged by order of the *Tziruf* / name-formation for that month (*Mishnas Chasidim,* Meseches Adar, 1:3). In addition to the order of the words and letters, the content meaning and greater context of the verse connected with each particular month is, of course, also part of the revelation of that month's guiding light.

The permutation of the Divine Name that we explored above comes from the last letters of the verse, *U-tzedakaH tihiyeH lanU kiY...* / "And it will be a merit to us if..." (*Devarim* 6:25). The verse continues, "...if we are careful to perform this entire command-ment before Hashem our G-d, as He has commanded us." This is part of the 'answer' that the Torah recommends we give if our child, the *Chacham* / wise one, asks us about the nature of the Torah's guidance. The *Chacham* also represents our own holy innocence and wisdom within. When this part of us is stimulated to actively seek out and articulate our deeper understanding, we realize with greater clarity that following the Torah's guidance brings us true merit and blessing in life. This realization further encourages us towards Teshuvah, since we all instinctively seek to increase merit and blessing in our lives.

The numerical value of these four words, without the four 'filling letters' (Hei, Hei, Yud and Vav), has the same numerical value as the word *beTeshuvah* / with (in) Teshuvah (*Bnei Yisaschar*, Elul 1). This alludes to the fact that Elul is an optimal time to make spiritual and behavioral breakthroughs with regard to Teshuvah. It is an op-portune time to gather in our entire past year and use it to come closer to Hashem, to seal it and kiss it goodbye.

Performing Teshuvah in Elul transforms the spiritual 'poverty' revealed in Tamuz and Av. We can see this fact through the lens of Gematria. The numerical sum of the first letter of each of the four words in this month's verse is 456 (Vav=6, Tav=400, Lamed=30, Chaf=20). This is the same numerical value as the sum of the words *Tamuz* (453) and *Av* (3). The final letters of these four words, as mentioned, form this month's letter-sequence of Hashem's name. Therefore, the final letters 'transform' the first letters. That is to say, the first letters of the verse represent a more 'external' or negative implication in the verse. We bring spiritual 'poverty' upon ourselves when we are not careful to live in accordance with Hashem's will. However, when we look beyond 'external' appearances and see the last letters of the verse, we find a more internal, positive implication in the verse: *b'Teshuvah*. With Teshuvah we can see the letters of Hashem's name hidden even within our mistakes and shortcomings — we therefore merit to behold Hashem's true presence within every dimension of creation. When we find this internal meaning within the verse, it transforms the external meaning; Teshuvah transforms spiritual poverty into a wealth of knowing the deeper reality of the Divine presence.

The word *u-Tzedakah* in our verse of course hints to the Mitzvah of charity, a powerful tool in the Teshuvah process (see, Rambam, *Hilchos Teshuvah*, 2:4). Increasing our charitable giving in this month will certainly help us transform our lives.

This period of 40 days, including the 30 days of Elul and the first 10 days of Tishrei through Yom Kippur, is the most appropriate and auspicious time for Teshuvah. This is because it is a cosmic time of Teshuvah and forgiveness mirroring Moshe's final 40 days on the Mountain following the episode of the Golden Calf. These 40 days of ultimate Teshuvah began on Rosh Chodesh Elul and culminated on Yom Kippur, when Moshe came down the Mountain with forgiveness for the people in the form of the second set of *Luchos* / Tablets.

First there is the Teshuvah of Elul, dealing with the old year and wrapping it up. Then begins the process of renewal with Rosh Hashanah, finally culminating with full forgiveness and re-creation on Yom Kippur.

LETTER

There are twenty-two letters in the Aleph Beis. As the Torah, which is the 'Blueprint of Creation,' is written in Hebrew, the *Lashon haKodesh* / Holy Tongue, the Sages teach that each of these twenty-two letters contain a host of metaphysical energies and creative potentials. According to the Sefer Yetzirah, a profound book of early Kabbalah that pays particular attention to the inner dimensions of the Hebrew letters, the twenty-two letters of the Aleph-Beis are divided into three categories: three "Mother Letters," seven "Double Letters," and twelve "Simple Letters." Each month is connected to one of the twelve Simple Letters.*

The letter associated with the month of Elul is Yud. The graphic design of the Yud is a small, elevated point. This is why Yud represents the *Nekudas haTov* / point of goodness, the *Pintele* or point of spiritual elevation within every person. It is the timeless purity of soul that remains unsullied within us, no matter how chaotic our outer life may seem.

In the language of the Zohar, Yud is called the *Nekudah Kadma'ah* / point of origin, the primal point through which all letters emanate. Just as Hei and Aleph are the origin of all vocal sounds or

---

* For a more in-depth analysis of all three categories of Hebrew letters and their relationship to the calendar, please see the introductory volume in this series: *The Spiral of Time: Unraveling the Yearly Cycle*.

'letters' of speech, Yud is the beginning of all written letters (*Zohar* 3, Achrei Mos, 78a. *Amud haAvodah*, "Kuntreisim leChochmas Emes", p. 328. The Aleph-Beis begins with the letter Aleph, but Aleph is comprised of a Yud below, a slanted Vav in the middle, and a Yud above. Yud is thus the beginning of the letter Aleph).

Graphically, Yud is the Nekudah of every *Os* / letter, the point from which every letter arises. When written out, the top of every letter of the Aleph-Beis originates with a small point resembling a Yud, and the body of the letter then extends downward and out-ward from this point (*Chesed l'Avraham*, Va'eschanan). The letter Yud is thus the prima materia of all the other letters. This is demonstrable by the fact that you must first touch the pen to paper in order to form a letter. At the very moment when the point of the pen makes contact with the writing surface, you have created a Yud.*

In fact, the letters that spell the word Yud (Yud-Vav-Dalet) can be rearranged to spell the word דיו / *D'yo* / ink. Yud is the drop of ink that starts every letter. These three letters are also a graphical display of expansion from a point to a line to an area. First there is a Yud a *Nekudah* / point (י), then this point extends down into a *Kav* / line (ו). Then finally the Dalet adds a horizontal vector and becomes a *Shetach* / area (ד) (Rebbe Rashab, *Sefer haMa'amarim* 5666 [Sa-mach Vav], B'Yom haShemini, p. 490. The Rebbe, *Basi l'Gani*, Lamed-Vav).

---

* According to the teachings of the AriZal, as revealed by Rabbi Yisrael Sarug, the "first" letter to emerge in Creation is the letter Yud, following what is called the *Tzimtzum* / contraction of the square. Within the "square" arose an *Avir Kadmon* /a primordial vapor and this Avir is also the *Ohr* / light of the Yud.

In other words, the Yud is the point that expands into manifestation, the small dot of ink, the pure potential that is expressed and articulated in each letter of creation.

This small point also alludes to the Nekudah Tovah within every 'letter' or manifestation in the world, including every experience that we perceive as negative. Through finding that inner point of goodness and expanding it, we can elevate and transform the negativity. This is an indispensable part of Teshuvah. We ourselves — all of our 'letters' or manifestations of self — begin with the Yud. Therefore, this primal point of goodness is always within us, even in negative states of thought and activity. We can always return to this point of goodness, since it is the place where our life originates at every moment.

The Yud is also our full potential before it is actualized. Say, for example, your name is Avraham. As you are living, you are *Avraham-ing*; your life is a process of becoming fully yourself, Avraham. In the moment of conception you were just a Yud, a potential 'Avraham.' No matter what happens in your life you can always go back to your original 'Yud,' and begin anew from that place of infinite potential.

Yud is the first letter of the four-letter Name of Hashem, and it corresponds to the attribute of *Chochmah* / imaginative or intuitive wisdom. When we look back on our past we can redeem it by finding the deeper wisdom and meaning within every experience. For example, if yesterday you spoke angrily to your co-worker, you can look for the wisdom hidden within such an unpleasant exchange: what was your higher self really asking for or pointing to in that moment? How can you meet that need now? Also, sometimes making amends with someone can make the relationship healthier than ever before. In this way, recovering the wisdom hidden in the event can help us move forward, make new choices, and forge deeper bonds. Elul is a perfect time to sift through your past to find the wisdom in it, and begin to redeem your whole life.

Just as Yud is the origin and potential of every letter, Chochmah is the origin and potential of all character traits and deeds, as expressed in the structure of the Sefiros. On the level of pure potentiality, anything can be actualized or transformed. By tapping into the deeper potential of Yud, one can take a particular letter and transform it into something different. With Chochmah, one can take a negative past and transform it into a positive future by doing Teshuvah and returning to your inner Yud in the present.

Everything is, in potential, perfectly good. Yud symbolizes *Olam haBa'a* / the world that is coming (*Menachos*, 29b. *Medrash Rabbah*, Bereishis, 12:10) — a future world where the potential of perfect goodness within all things is revealed. This future world corresponds to the *Pintele* within us where everything is already perfect. By tapping back into our *Pintele* and transforming ourselves through *Teshuvah*, we help bring a future of revealed goodness for all creation.

Originally, the three intense summer months of Tamuz, Av, and Elul were in the domain of Eisav, meaning the forces of *Tohu* / confusion and chaos. Yet, Yaakov, the side of *Kedusha* / holiness, was able to wrestle half of Av and the whole month of Elul away from the clutches of the negative side and transform them into positivity.

Elul, as mentioned, is connected with the letter Yud, and specifically with the Yud of Yaakov. The name Yaakov is spelled with the letter *Yud* plus the word *Eikev* / heel. When Yaakov is born he receives this name because his 'hand,' his *Yad* (or Yud), was holding onto Eisav's heel (*Bereishis*, 25:26).

Theoretically, Yaakov could have been called *Eikev*, without the Yud in the beginning of his name. This would have been a reference to the 'heel' without the 'hand.' There is also something peculiar with the name Eisav. The name עשו / Eisav comes from the word עשוי / *Asui* / made or completed. Rashi (*ibid*, 25:25) explains that the name *Eisav* represents the fact that he was born like a finished product, especially with regard to his hair, which covered his entire body from birth. But the word for an object being finished is *Asui*, which includes a Yud at the end. Just as Yaakov seems to have an added Yud in the beginning of his name, Eisav seems to be missing a Yud at the end of his name. This dynamic suggests that Yaakov took Eisav's Yud (*Megaleh Amukos*, Bechukosai, 51), which represents the absorbing of Elul into the domain of Yaakov, the domain of Kedusha.

Practically this means that we can retrieve the Yud of ultimate wisdom even from deep within the darkness and the lowest of places within our lives. This is the deep work of Teshuvah we need to do in Elul, looking back into our past year and redeeming everything from the 'other side.' We have to learn from all our experiences, and derive wisdom from our past mistakes.

No matter how difficult a challenge may be, whether it be a lost job, a broken relationship, or even the death of a loved one — if we wish to live in the present with wisdom, we need to learn to ask productive questions. For instance, it is not necessarily productive to ask, "*Why* did this happen to me?" Nor does it help to explain a negative situation away by blaming it on external causes. A better question is *What* — 'What could I possibly learn from this situation?' or 'What is the deeper meaning of this event?' Perhaps you will realize that, 'This is happening now so that I can learn something for the future.'

When we ask 'Why' in an attempt to find a logical reason or cause for events in our life or in history, we are focussing solely on the past and thus living in the past. For some people, this focus becomes an obsessive-compulsive fixation on the past. We can never truly know 'why' things happen. Only the Creator knows every side of the story, the hidden causes and reasons. Knowledge that is existentially relevant to our lives is knowledge of what is existing now and what patterns may play out in the future.

Instead of focusing on the *Lamah* / why, we should train ourselves to focus on the *leMah* / towards what end. Rather than trying to trace an event's 'genealogy,' we should try to intuit the potential trajectory of the event in the present. We should resist the illusion of false certainty within mythological histories, and remain vulnerable and open to the infinite possibilities of the future by being fully present in the now. When we ask, 'Why' we are looking to lay blame for something that is past, something that no longer exists. When we ask, 'towards what end' we are claiming responsibility for the co-creation of what does exist: the now and potential future 'now.'

NAME OF THE MONTH

*A*CCORDING TO THE TORAH, NAMES ARE VERY POWERFUL (*Yumah*, 83b. *Tanchuma*, Hazinu. *Berachos*, 7b). Comprised as they are of Hebrew letters, they represent and define the energy or attributes of that which is named (*Tanya*, Sha'ar HaY-ichud Veha'emunah, 1). Our names, for instance, unlock and reveal hidden potentials present within our own spiritual makeup. Similarly, names of other people, places, and periods of time provide subtle hints as to their deeper purpose or poetic significance. Additionally, changing one's name is akin to a kind of rebirth; some might even say that a change of name initiates a change of *Mazal* (*Rashi*, Bereishis 15:5. *Rosh Hashanah*, 16b. *Yerushalmi*, Shabbos, 6:39. *Ramah*, Yoreh Deah, 335:10).

Each of the twelve months of the year has a distinct name, and every name has a meaning. According to our Sages, the current names we have for the months were imported to our tradition upon our return to Israel from the Babylonian Exile (They can in fact be traced to ancient Babylonian or Akkadian names. See *Yerushalmi*, Rosh Hashanah, 1:2. *Medrash Rabbah*, Bereishis, 48:9). In the times before the Babylonian Exile, the names of the months were mostly known by their number in the sequence of the year. For example, the month of Av was called "the Fifth Month," and Cheshvan was known as "the Eighth Month."

Accordingly, prior to the Babylonian Exile, this month was known simply as, "the Sixth Month." Following the rebuilding of the Beis HaMikdash, however, we see that this month is called Elul (*Nechemya*, 6:5). The Akkadian name for this month was *Ululu*, which in Canaanite means to 'ululate' or shout for joy (and it may also be related to the French phrase, *ooh là là*). These meanings, which indicate a lightness of spirit, seem to contrast with the teachings of our Sages, who suggest that the word *Elul* is connected with an Aramaic word meaning 'to carefully search.' What is the connection?

Moshe sent the spies to the Land of Israel in order to לתור אתה /Lasur Osa / to search it out (*Bamidbar*, 13:32). The Targum translates this phrase as לאללא יתה / l'Alalah Yasa. The word l'Alalah is connected to the word *Elul*. This suggests (*Toldas Adam*, Ki Savo, in the name of Rabbi Chayim Vital), that in Elul we should embark upon a search, and specifically in the mode of *Lasur* (or in Sephardic pronunciation *Latur* — like a *Tur* / a tourist). A tourist searches out and researches a foreign land carefully, but also with great interest and energy. Elul is thus a month of soul-searching, as the Sages teach, but this should be done with a sense of purpose and joy, and with an attitude that we will overcome our challenges. Teshuvah is a Mitzvah and like all Mitzvos it should be done with intention, determination, and joy.

To illustrate: *One day in Elul, the Baal Shem Tov visited a town where the congregation recited the penitential Selichos service with exuberant rejoicing. The Baal Shem Tov asked them, "Please tell me why you are so full of joy. Don't most people weep when reciting these prayers?" They answered him, "Rebbe, when a person is cleaning his home in preparation for the imminent visit of the King, how could he not rejoice?"*

In Elul we are called to clean our internal house and search our internal 'land' with joy, as if with an ululation. Then we are to own all of our past, discern its trajectory for the future, integrate its wisdom, and kiss it good-bye.

The numerical value of the word *Elul*, in *Mispar Katan* / small numbers (in which all numbers are reduced to their single decimal count) is 13. Throughout Elul, the Thirteen Attributes of Divine Mercy are in a process of revelation which culminates with the last prayer of Yom Kippur.

The *Gematria* / numerical value of *Elul* is 67, which is the same value as the word *Binah* / understanding. Binah is the quality of the higher Hei of Hashem's name. Binah also alludes to *Teshuvah Ila'ah*, the higher Teshuvah, and the transformation of our consciousness, our 'understanding' of life. Adding '1' for the value of the word itself, the extended value of *Elul* is 68 — the same as the word *Chayim* / life (Chidah, *Nachal Eshkol*, Shir HaShirim, 6:3), alluding to the fact that Teshuvah, the primary spiritual work of Elul, gives us life and hope for a better future.

The letters of the word *Elul* are also an acronym for the phrase אני לדודי ודודי לי

/ *Ani L'dodi V'dodi Li* / I am to my Beloved and my Beloved is to me (*Shir Hashirim*, 6:3. AriZal, *Sha'ar HaPesukim*, on this Pasuk. *Audaraham*, Seder Tefilos, Rosh Hashanah. *Bach*, Orach Chayim, 581). This phrase describes a movement from below (the Hei) to Above — in Elul we work to raise ourselves upward towards our Divine Beloved, the Giver. This, again, is the paradigm of Teshuvah. The month of Nisan, by contrast is the season of miracles and a downward movement from our Beloved toward us: "My Beloved is to me, and I am to Him" (*Shir Hashirim*, 2:16).

Notably, Yud is the last letter in each of the four words in the phrase *Ani L'dodi V'dodi Li*. The numerical value of Yud is 10, these four Yuds thus equal 40 (as the *Bach*, ibid mentions). As mentioned, Forty alludes to the 30 days of Elul and the Ten Days of Repentance culminating with Yom Kippur. These are known as 'the Final Days' when full Teshuvah was granted to the People of Israel in the Desert, and when it is still granted to us today.

To become *Tahor* / ritually pure, one of the goals of complete Teshuvah, a person must immerse in a Mikvah, or ritual bath. In a Mikvah there are a minimum of 40 *Sa'ah* of water, (*Yuma*, 31a. *Eiruvin*, 4b. This measurement is Torah law. *Teshuvas HaRivash*, 294), corresponding to the forty days of Teshuvah.

Generally, according to Halacha, something is *Batel* / nullified when it is no more than one part in 60. The body is comprised of four basic primordial elements (fire, wind, water and earth), and each element has within it the other three, so in fact there are 16 sub-elements in the body. The 16 elements, multiplied by the 60 parts, equal 960. In 40 *Sa'ah* there are 960 *Lugin*. Therefore, the body is *Batel B'shishim* / nullified in sixty when immersed in the 960 Lugin of the Mikvah.

Now, each of the forty days from the beginning of Elul until Yom Kippur is comprised of 24 hours, and 40 x 24 = 960. This is another hint alluding to the fact that this period is a *Mikvah within time.*[*] To immerse yourself completely in the spirit of Elul is to be nullified within the purity of the Divine Presence. Ultimately Elul is about reorienting ourselves, changing the direction of our lives so that we live consciously and with awareness of being in the presence of the True King, who is in fact smiling at us, as will be explained shortly.

Beyond the verse from Song of Songs mentioned above, the letters of Elul (Aleph-Lamed-Vav-Lamed) are an acronym for a variety of verses, including the ones listed below. Each verse alludes to a specific dimension of spiritual work that we can increase and improve during Elul:

---

* *B'nei Yisaschar*, Elul, Ma'amor 1:15. Indeed, the essence of each Mitzvah can be activated within any of the three realms of *Olam*, *Shanah*, and *Nefesh* — 'space,' 'time,' and 'consciousness.' Thus, there can be a Mikvah in time, just as there is in space. To learn more about this idea, please see the book, *The Secrets of the Mikvah: Waters of Transformation*.

1) *"Ani L'dodi V'dodi Li* / I am to my Beloved and my Beloved is to me"* (*Shir Hashirim*, 6:3). This verse alludes to *Tefilah* / prayer, reaching up from below to Above.

2) "Then Hashem your God will open up (literally, 'circumcise') *Es L'vavcha, V'es L'vav...* / your heart and the hearts [of your off-spring]" (*Devarim*, 30:6. Ba'al HaTurim, ad loc. Bach, ibid). This alludes to Teshuvah and spiritual transformation, the opening of our hearts.

3) "The sending of portions (of food) *Ish L're'eihu, U-matonas L'evyonim* / to one's friends, and gifts to the needy" (*Esther* 9:22). This alludes to *Tzedakah* / charity and helping others in need (*Arugas Habosem* and *Eliya Rabbah*, 581).

4) *"Ina L'yado V'samti Lach* / And for one who did not lie in wait [to kill premeditatedly], but Hashem has caused it to happen, I shall establish for you a place [to which he can flee] (*Shemos*, 21:13. *Pri Eitz Chayim*, Sha'ar Rosh Hashanah, 1). This verse refers to the Mitzvah of building cities of refuge, which alludes to Torah-study — a refuge for the soul.

5) *"Echad Leolah, V'echad Lachatas* / One will be for the burnt offering and the other for the purification offering" (*Vayikra*, 12:8). This verse refers to sacrifices brought to the Holy Temple, which allude inwardly to the concept of *Mesiras Nefesh* / self-sacrifice, dedicating and offering our inner 'animal' on the Altar.

6) "Then Moshe and the Israelites sang *Es* this song *LaHashem, Vayomru Leimor* / to Hashem, and they said" (*Shemos*, 15:1. *Shulchan Aruch HaArizal*, Elul). This acronym skips two words. Or the four letters of Elul in this verse are actually in reverse order, in the words

LaHashem, Vayomru, Leimor, Ashira. In any case, this verse alludes to the *Simcha* / joy of liberation and redemption. Each dimension of our spiritual work during Elul must be infused with joy.

☾

ꙮ
SENSE

*T*HE CONVENTIONAL WORLD IDENTIFIES FIVE SENSES, YET *Sefer Yetzirah* speaks of twelve *Chushin* / senses. In addition to the more commonly understood definition of what comprises our 'senses,' the word *chush* can also mean, 'a sensitive level of perception, understanding, appreciation, and skill' in relation to a particular process or function. For example, a 'sense of sleep' is a deep understanding and appreciation of sleep which includes both: A) what sleep represents spiritually, as well as, B) the practical skills and abilities that make one's experience of sleep both peaceful and restorative.

These twelve *Chushim* are also the twelve activities that the Torah describes the Creator performing in the perpetual process of maintaining the world (*Pirush haRavad, Sefer Yetzirah*). As we are created in the Divine image we also possess all twelve *Chushim*, at least in potential.* Every month gives us the ability and strength to expand our vessels (potentials) for a particular *Chush*, along with its corresponding Divine Attributes. When we align and refine our consciousness via these *Chushim*, we can harness the qualities of each month in a most profound and meaningful way.

The *Chush* / sense of Elul is *Asiyah* / action or making. The Chush of action is embodied in a person who is a 'doer' or a 'fixer.' This trait is appropriate for the process of Teshuvah and making a *Tikkun* / fixing in one's life. Moshe himself exemplified the sense of Asiyah after the sin of the golden calf, when he responded to the Divine instruction to "make" or carve the second *Luchos* / Tablets as the final expression of his 40 days of Teshuvah (*Shemos*, 34:1). This, too, occurred during the month of Elul (*Pirush HaGra*, Sefer Yetzirah 5:9). Since merely changing our 'mind-state' or our 'lives' in general may not transform us, we can assume that the mode of Asiyah highlighted during this month specifically refers to the repetitive performance of specific, positive actions that are eventually 'carved' into our psyche until they become our new inner reality, similar to the way Moshe 'carved' the letters of the 10 Commandments into the second Luchos.

---

* Even if one is blind, for example, he always has the *potential* for sight — it's just that he is currently missing the physical vessels (capacity) for it (*Pirush HaGra*, Hakdamah, *Sefer Yetzirah*). However, the sense of sight is included in the person's Divine image, as it were. Obviously, a physically blind person could have immense vessels for spiritual sight.

Many people, when they look at their lives, experience a general feeling of unhappiness, boredom, despair or disgust. They feel the need to make drastic changes in order to balance out their existential equation. If they feel *this* bad, then they need to do something equally or exceptionally major to make themselves feel *that* good. And so they dream big and they shoot for the stars. This is not bad in and of itself. It is just that to undo a negative pattern of behavior, it is not enough to know that it's a wrong behavior.

Let's say a person feels like they need to become a better spouse, and so resolves, 'From now on, I am going to be the best spouse in the world.' While this may be a genuine sentiment it may only produce a few days of exaggerated niceties or more quality time with one's spouse. But then, sadly, the old habits will most likely reassert themselves if approached in this manner. The goal itself is good, but simply making a declaration does not work because: A) it does not address all the practicalities; the declaration is very general and the old patterns of behavior are very specific. B) the reactive behaviors remain undisturbed as one's underlying habits, and it is only natural to return to ingrained habits.

A resolution is therefore not *the* solution, although it is a first step. To actually rewire the brain and program new habitual behaviors we need to convert our general resolutions into specific, practical, repetitive actions.

For this reason it would be much more effective to say, "Every day when I come home, I will give my spouse 15 uninterrupted minutes of my time;" or, "Next time I go out with my spouse I will not look at my text messages for the first half hour." Such practical small actions and responses, when repeated over and over again, will eventually set up new patterns of behavior in the brain.

Tamuz corresponds to the sense of *Re'iya* / seeing, and Av to *Shemi'a* / hearing. These two Hebrew words begin with the letters Reish and Shin, which together spell the word רש / *Rash* / deprived or poor, as those two months are considered, at least on the surface, to be spiritually 'deprived' of goodness. *Asiyah* begins with the letter Ayin, and when this letter is added to Reish and Shin, it spells the word שער / *Sha'ar* / gate. Elul is the Sha'ar that closes the past year, and opens to the goodness of the year to come, allowing any 'deprivations of goodness' in the past year to be transformed and evolved as we transform and evolve through Teshuvah.

When the Divine name *Adon-ai* is spelled out in full (spelling the names of the letters Aleph-Dalet-Nun-Yud), there are 12 letters corresponding to the 12 months of the year (according to the count of months starting in Nisan).* Tamuz and Av are the fourth and fifth months/letters in this sequence (Dalet and Lamed) and Elul is the sixth month/letter (Tav). The letters Dalet-Lamed spell דל /*Dal*, another word for 'poor,' alluding to the negative spiritual quality of Tamuz and Av. However, when we add the Tav of Elul, the word *Dal* becomes the word דלת /*Deles* / door. Again, Elul is the door (or gate) that closes on the past year and opens to new possibilities for the coming year. The practices of Elul help us to specify, own, and achieve closure on the negativity of our past. Then we can step forward into a new space, time, and soul.

---

* These are 1) Aleph, 2) Lamed, 3) Pei, 4) Dalet, 5) Lamed, 6) Tav, 7) Nun, 8) Vav, 9) Nun, 10) Yud, 11) Vav, and 12) Dalet.

As mentioned, the letter of the month is Yud, which represents the realm of thought, yet, the sense of the month is in the realm of action. Thought and action seem to be opposites, and so there seems to be a contradiction in the theme of Elul. But this is because "The beginning is wedged in the end" (*Sefer Yetzirah* 1:7). In the beginning of the year we are inspired and we have a plan, a thought of how the year should unfold, what we will accomplish and how we will grow. At the end of the year there is a culmination of our plans in action.

To illustrate: You have an idea or vision of how your home will look before you start building it. However, only once you have completed building the home, can you say, 'This is exactly how I envisioned it.' In the same way, Elul is both a month of thought and of action.

On a deeper level, Elul is a month of Teshuvah, a time where our thoughts are reckoned against, reconciled, and finally reunified with our actions. When our lived actions are the direct materialization of our envisioned thoughts, then our actions/life and thoughts/dreams are one.

☾

♈

SIGN

*E*ACH MONTH CONTAINS THE ZODIAC INFLUENCE OF A PARTICU-
LAR constellation, called the *Mazal*. A constellation is comprised of a perceivably patterned grouping of visible stars.
Today, we count 88 constellations in the night sky. Out of all of
these, one constellation is predominantly visible on the horizon at
the beginning of each month.

Each constellation refracts the light of the cosmos differently,
alternately reflecting times that are more conducive to war, and

times that are more conducive for peace, for example (*Yalkut Reuveini, Bereishis,* Oys 56). Additionally, the *Zohar* teaches that each sign can manifest positively or negatively (*Zohar* 3, 282a). In other words, the quality of a constellation can have either a productive or a destructive influence in one's life, depending on how we process its energy. It is important to keep in mind, however, that even if our proclivities are innate or celestially influenced, we still possess the freedom to choose how we respond to the situations that arise in our life. In other words, we have the ability to consciously reflect back what has been projected onto us, even if from the stars. For example, a person born under the influence of Mars may have a tendency to be drawn towards blood, but he or she also has the ability to employ this inherent tendency for good or ill; such a person could therefore choose to be a violent criminal or a life-saving surgeon (*Shabbos,* 156a).

Due to the prevailing popular belief that the stars exert a kind of fatalistic influence upon world history and human development, we need to repeatedly emphasize that anyone can rise above these influences altogether and be unaffected by them. Despite all the forces and influences in our life — physical and psychological conditions, upbringing, education, environment, financial status, etc. — we always have the freedom to choose. Simply put: we have the choice to live as either the *effect* of our conditions (as passive receivers of what life serves us), or as the *cause* of what comes next, thereby becoming proactive co-creators of our lives. When we begin to live more proactively, the influences of our birth constellation, as well as the *Mazal* of each month, function less as positive or negative *influences*; they become as *tools* that can help us climb ever higher into our freedom of being.

The constellation of Elul is *Besulah* / virgin, corresponding to the Zodiac sign of Virgo.* The 'Elul' within each person is the state of 'virginal purity,' the deeper essence of the soul, that remains untouched by any action or inaction. This is the inner Yud, as discussed, which is always with us. This is the origin and the goal of Teshuvah. The word *Teshuvah* does not actually mean repentance; it comes from the word *Shuv* / return, implying that Teshuvah is a process of returning to the root of your soul, to the core of who you truly are (The Rebbe, *Likutei Sichos*, 2, p. 409). Our Tikkun is to return to our essence. In fact, the letters that make up the word *Tikkun* can be rearranged to spell the word *Tinok* / child to return to our essence is to reconnect to the inner child within who is always whole and perfect. Our task in Elul is precisely to reclaim our integral wholeness and essential purity.

Virgos tend to be introspective, disciplined, and emotionally conservative. They also seek attention less than Leos do. Virgos are good observers, and can remain emotionally detached. They are born with a natural tendency to actively serve and help others, and are often doctors, social workers and bankers.

The first time we find the word *Besulah* in the Torah is in relation to Rivka (*Bereishis*, 24:16). She is the one who gives birth to the twins Eisav and Yaakov.

---

* *Bereishis*, 6:2 refers to the "Daughters of Adam" stating clearly that they "were good." The *Rosh* says in the name of the Medrash that this means they were 'good and beautiful in actions.' When the 'sons of Elokim' said to her, "Listen to us," she replied, "I will, but only if you give me your wings." Whereupon she flew with her wings to the Heavens above and held onto the Throne of Glory. The Creator then received her and placed her among the constellations; this is the Mazal of *Besulah* / Virgo. *Pirush haRosh, Pirushei haRishonim al haTorah.*

Yaakov represents the 'revealed' Tzadik or the path of perfection, and Eisav represents the potential Baal Teshuvah, the one who must struggle to return to wholeness along a more winding path full of mistakes and seeming detours. These two brothers are similar to the Rambam's description of the חסיד המעולה / *Chasid haMe'ula* / the perfect Chasid, or one who is illumined from birth, and the person who is הכובש את יצרו / *haKovesh Es Yitzro* / the imperfect one who conquers his temptations (*Shemona Pirakim*, 6). Both of these paradigms are included within the *Besulah*, the pure soul-essence within us, which remains perfect no matter what. If we have made mistakes in the past year, we can through Teshuvah, now return to this inner purity, and draw forth from it the energy of our inner Tzadik and our inner Baal Teshuvah.

Yaakov is called *Tam* (*Bereishis*, 25:27), the 'perfect' or 'wholesome' one who dwells in the tents of Torah study. He is the embodiment of the energy of *Tikkun* / rectification, meaning the harmony, stability, and orderliness of integrated vessels. Eisav, on the other hand, is a wildly hairy man who spent his time hunting in the fields. He is the embodiment of *Tohu* / chaos, the volatility (and potential) of uncontained, ungrounded spiritual energy.

Yaakov and Eisav are also comparable to the two sets of Luchos, the Tablets of Torah revealed at Sinai. The first Luchos, which were given in the month of Sivan, were broken in Tamuz. Because they were broken, they represent the energy of Eisav and Tohu. We come to the month of Elul as a potential Baal Teshuvah, admitting the chaos of our past, finding the positive wisdom within our mistakes, and seeking to reconnect with our inner purity.

The second set of Luchos were given during the forty days of Teshuvah from Elul through Yom Kippur. These Tablets were lasting, because the energy of Tohu was contained and supported within the vessels of Tikkun. This illustrates the value of Teshuvah — it can give birth to a 'positive chaos,' as it were, harnessing the raw power of Eisav for ultimate goodness. The key is to 'be' Rivka, the Besulah who includes, integrates, and gives birth to the energies of both her sons. Then, like Yaakov, we can reabsorb the Yud from the chaotic domain of Eisav and bring it back into Kedusha and Tikkun. This is our opportunity in Elul, summed up by the popular teaching that during Elul, the King is in the field (*Likutei Torah*, Re'eh, 32b). During Elul, we are thus able to meet our inner Eisav on his own turf, so to speak, in the field, in order to hunt and gather any fallen sparks from our past year. Only then can we reintegrate and recycle this misdirected energy for a higher purpose, bringing all aspects of ourselves back into the tent of Torah.

If we rearrange the letters of the word *Elul*, it spells *El Lamed-Vav* / to the 36. In Elul, we move inward, toward our inner '36' — the spiritual light of creation that shone openly for Adam and Chavah throughout their 36 hours in the Garden of Eden. After they left the Garden, however, this light was concealed as the *Ohr haGanuz* / Hidden Light. Where was this pristine light hidden? It was hidden within the Torah (*Zohar* 1, 47a), and deeply within each one of us. When we do Teshuvah, we turn inward and move towards our true core, where we can reveal the holy light of who we really are.

The numerical value of the word *Elul* is 67, which equals the 29 days of the month of Elul, plus the 30 days of Tishrei, plus the 7 first days of Cheshvan, plus 1 for this whole period as a unit. In ancient Israel, on the seventh day of Cheshvan, the pilgrims began to pray for rain (Mishnah, *Ta'anis*, 10a), since this was the date when the last Israelite to leave the Festival celebrations in Jerusalem would finally arrive home. The Alter Rebbe writes in Shulchan Aruch (*Orach Chayim*, 117:1), "In Israel we begin to ask for rain starting from the Seventh of Cheshvan.... It would really have been fitting to ask for rain immediately after Sukkos, however they delayed asking for 15 days following the Festival, so that the last person in Israel, from the Temple for the Festival, should reach his home — even if it was near the Pras River, the settlement furthest from Jerusalem."

The end goal of Elul, and all of these 67 days, is to bring us home to the stainless essence of who we are, and then to live from that place of purity amid the mundane concerns of daily life, such as 'tending to our crops' or making a living.

☾

♈

TRIBE

*E*VERY MONTH OF THE YEAR IS CONNECTED WITH ONE OF the Twelve Tribes of Israel, the sons of Yaakov (*Sefer Yetzirah*; Medrash, *Osyos Rebbe Akiva*, Dalet).

Gad is the tribe associated with the month of Elul. In general, the word *Gad* means 'camp' (*Bereishis*, 49:19). The special talent of Gad was to organize a 'company' of warriors. Gad also means 'good Mazal' or good fortune (*Bereishis*, 30:11). When Gad was born, his mother Leah said, "*Ba Gad* / Now good Mazal has come" (See *Rashi* on Bereishis, 30:11, quoting *Medrash Rabbah*, 71:9. See also the *Targum Yonason Ben Uziel*). Gad is also connected to the "Gate of *Kavod* / honor" (*Nesiv Mitzvosecha*, Nesiv Emunah, Shevil 3), and as we mentioned earlier, Kavod is connected to Elul.

Numerically the value of Gad is 7: Gimel (3) plus Dalet (4). Gad was the seventh son to be born to Yaakov. The name Gad is encoded within the concept of Mazal and good fortune. The word *Mazal* is composed of the letters Mem (40), Zayin (7), and Lamed (30). The Gimel of *Gad* is 3, but as a 'full array' this number is multiplied by ten, becoming 30, matching the letter Lamed of Mazal. The Dalet of Gad is 4, and as a 'full array' is 40, matching the letter Mem of Mazal. The simple value of *Gad* (7) matches the Zayin of Mazal. We could thus say the full extension of the concept of *Gad* is *Mazal*, or Gad is a condensation of the energy of good Mazal.

In general, *Mazal* means a constellation of stars. Based on the alignment of the zodiac (which is an external expression of the internal Divine reality being revealed at a particular moment), a person born at a particular hour on a particular day is prone to receive certain blessings based on the position of the stars at that moment; this is Mazal.

According to Rabbi Yochanan, "there is no Mazal for Israel" (*Shabbos*, 156a). Yet, the Gemara also says, "Life, children, and wealth depend on Mazal" (*Moed Katan*, 28a. Although see the Meiri, *ad loc*). Many sages also say that through Torah-study and acts of *Zechus* / merit, one's Mazal can change (*Tosefos*, Moed Katan, 28a. *Tosefos*, Kidushin, 82b. See also Maharsha, ibid. Maharal, *Chidushei Agadas* Shabbos, 156a). Therefore, "no Mazal" does not mean a total absence of Mazal, it means that through our study and prayer we have the *Koach* / power to reach a level above Mazal, and access the Infinite Source of all good fortune. This is the power of true free-will when directed by Torah.

Mazal means a *Shefa* / abundance that is *Nozel* / flowing from the Heavens above to the world below. The deeper aspect of *Gad* is also associated with the continuity of flow, movement from one place or dimension to another.

When the letters Gimel and Daled appear in a word in this sequence, the word often refers to a continuation, extension, or grouping.* For example, אגודה אחת *Aguda Achas* / one congregation, or לא תתגודדו /*Lo Tisgodedu* / do not make factions (the prohibition of making differentiated groups in the community). Even in the language of Chazal, Gad means connecting or continuation, as in the phrases גוד אסיק /*Gud Asik* and גוד אחית /*Gud Achis* / a wall extending upwards and a wall extending downwards. Homiletically, the sequence of Gimel and Daled suggests the 'extension' of a *Gomel* / giver toward a *Dal* / poor person or receiver (*Shabbos*, 104a). The Torah calls the *Mon* / Manna, "seed of *Gad*." Why? "Because *Mon* is like a tale, which (connects to and) draws the heart of man like water" (*Shemos*, 16:31. *Yuma*, 75a).

The tribe of Gad was called a *Marchiv* / an expanding tribe (*Devarim*, 33:20). This is because the tribe of Gad expanded the preliminary boundaries of Eretz Yisrael, to connect to and include the eastern side of the Jordan river, as part of the greater, future Eretz Yisrael.

---

* Parenthetically, Gad can also connote the exact opposite, 'to cut off' (*Daniel*, 4:11), as it also means a border, such as in the word *Geder* / fence, boundary. Interestingly, the word *Gad* also connotes *Avodah Zarah* / idol worship. In the Gemara (*Shabbos*, 67b), the term *Avodah Zarah* implies a type of inner separation.

In Elul, we are connecting with our entire past year (including our mistakes and missteps), finding the deeper wisdom in it, and using it all to return to our essential purity. By doing so we are *Marchiv* / expanding the boundaries of Kedusha in our lives. This higher level of Teshuvah transforms past intentional sins and chaos into merits as Tikkun.

In order to accomplish this, you need to be strong. Accordingly, the tribe of Gad included mighty warriors (*Rashi, Devarim*, 33:21), who would be the first to go out to battle on the front lines. To be a righteous and holy person you must be a spiritual warrior and fight for what you believe in and how you truly want to live your life. You must not give up or become lethargic when this becomes difficult. When you fall down, pick yourself up right away and continue marching forward. Expansion and perpetual growth, which are cornerstones of Torah, demand principled perseverance.

The tribe of Gad decided to settle on the east side of the Jordan River outside of the Biblical boundaries of Eretz Yisrael. This allowed them to form a גדר / *Geder* / fence or buffer to protect the Land from intruding enemies. Establishing and maintaining a beneficial Geder involves spiritual sensitivity and awareness of our boundaries. Through the work of Teshuvah, we gather in and connect to the good points of our past (our talents, gifts, sense of humor, and essential nature) in order to find our true place in life and learn how to protect it by erecting a healthy Geder around it. This prevents any intruding narratives of our past from impinging on our expanding Kedusha in the present.

Gad and the Focusing of the Subconscious

Elul is connected with rectifying the subconscious mind, and learning to redirect and focus our actions. This is the goal of Teshuvah — to consciously repair that which we have unconsciously ruined. Lack of integrity on a subconscious level is the root-cause of unintentional, mindless behavior. Gad is also connected with this concept, as we will see.

The highest level of *Yichud* / intimacy with one's spouse is to be totally present with and focused on them, not thinking of anybody else in the world (*Nedarim*, 20b). In any type of human interaction, it is most beneficial to be fully present and mindful of that person when interfacing or communicating with them.

In the story of the birth of Gad, there is something peculiar. When Yaakov is intimate with Gad's mother, Zilpah, the Torah says simply, "*vaTeiled...* / Leah's servant Zilpah bore Yaakov a son"(*Bereishis*, 30:9). With regard to all the other mothers it says *veTahar* / "she became pregnant." Why does the Torah omit the fact of pregnancy in the case of Gad?

The Megaleh Amukos (*Megaleh Amukos*, Matos, Derush 4), reveals that Yaakov was intimate with Zilpah without *Shiduchim* / engagement or courting. Therefore, the Torah does not say, "And he came unto her, and she became pregnant," only that "Zilpah bore Yaakov a son." But still this requires explanation.

If we look closely at the narrative we can understand that Yaakov lived with Bilhah, Rachel's maidservant, because Rachel was not, at that point, able to have any children. According to ancient

Near Eastern family structures, by having children with Bilhah, it was like having children with Rachel. And so, Yaakov lived with Bilhah and had children. But then why did Yaakov need to have children with Zilpah, Leah's maidservant, as he had already had many children with Leah? The Torah says, "When Leah saw that she had stopped having children, she took her servant Zilpah and gave her to Yaakov as a wife" (*Bereishis*, 30:9). Leah desired as many children as possible, and so she pushed Yaakov to be intimate with Zilpah, even though he had no or little interest.

There is a fascinating Medrash to support this idea. The Medrash teaches that Leah, perhaps knowing that Yaakov had little interest in Zilpah, dressed her up that evening in her own garments (just like Rachel did with Leah on the first night of her marriage to Yaakov). "And when Yaakov was with her, he thought he was with Leah, as Zilpah was made to look as Leah" (Medrash, see *Torah Sheleima*, Bereishis, 30:11). In other words, Yaakov was not consciously thinking of Zilpah when he was with her.

When the child from that eventful evening was born, Leah proclaimed, "*Ba Gad.*" This is translated as 'good Mazal,' but it also alludes to the Hebrew word *Bagad* / treason or deceit. The very identity of Gad was thus that he was conceived in *Bagad* (*Rashi*, ad loc). Accordingly, as Gad was conceived in unfocused intimacy, a type of unintentional action, descendants (genealogical or spiritual) of this tribe struggle with 'unintentional accidents.' Thus, in proportion to the general population, there were more 'cities of refuge' for people who kill by accident on the east side of the Jordan River than in Eretz Yisrael proper, as there are more accidents there (According to Chazal, there were also more intentional killings there as well. See *Makos*, 9b,

Tosefos, "beGilad." *Gur Aryeh* (Maharal), Bamidbar, 35:14). Being prone to accidents, in general, suggests a type of haphazard, unfocused approach to living.

The Tikkun of Gad involved generating the total focus and clarified presence that was missing at his conception. We too, especially in Elul, need to examine our lack of focus and presence in our relationships and actions. We need to gather all our divergent subconscious thoughts, energies, inclinations and desires that distract us from being present, and focus all of that chaotic energy into mindful actions of love and connection. We need to relate to others actively and with sensitive awareness, without inner distraction or deceit.

The ultimate and final ingathering of all exilic reality will be with the coming of Moshiach who will be heralded by *Eliyahu ha-Navi* / Elijah the Prophet. Eliyahu, by some accounts, is from the tribe of Gad (*Medrash Rabba*, Bereishis, 71:12). He will come "to inspire Israel to be upright and prepare their hearts... not to declare the pure, impure, or to declare the impure, pure... rather, he will establish peace within the world" (Rambam, *Hilchos Melachim*, 12:2). May it be speedily in our days, *Amein*.

☾

℘
BODY PART

ℰACH MONTH IS CONNECTED WITH THE GENERAL ENERGY and particular vibration of a specific body part. This empowers us to focus on and refine the spiritual properties and miraculous functionings of our physical bodies, as the spiral of the yearly cycle continues to turn on its Divine axis.

The body part associated with Elul is the left hand.* Since the majority of people are right-handed, the left hand is a universal symbol of our weaker side, and the subconscious mind.** However, a right-handed person can strengthen their left hand through repeated exercise and articulation. So too, we can reprogram our

---

* The left hand, says the Zohar is the holy *Yonah* / dove (*Tikunei Zohar*, 9a). This also corresponds to the final letter Hei in Hashem's name. Throughout *Shir haShirim* / Song of Songs, the bride (which is Klal Yisrael) is compared to a dove (see also *Shir HaShirim Rabbah*, 1:15. *Berachos*, 53b).

**With the exception of a few customs, a left-handed person regards their *right hand* as their "left" or weaker hand. For our discussion, left-handers can simply reverse the terms "left" and "right" (although the characteristics of the left and right brain hemispheres may remain the same for everyone).

unconscious mind with 'Teshuvah through action.' The spiritual effect of repeated 'action' can change the patterned functioning of the subconscious mind and strengthen our ability to act with sensitivity and compassion.

According to a perhaps oversimplified scientific theory, the articulation of the left hand is connected to activity in the right hemisphere of the brain. In general, the right hemisphere is associated with the powers of imagination and Chochmah (the Yud). As we have described, Teshuvah is designed to purify the imagination and positively transform the inner psyche of a person.

The left hand represents actions that are perpetuated without conscious thought, either by routine or subconscious reaction. However, these almost entirely reactive behaviors are entrained by repeated decisions and actions that become wired into the right hemisphere — itself a more reactive, less analytical part of the brain. By choosing new repetitive, 'left-handed' actions we can gradually build new circuitry in the right hemisphere and transform the functioning of our instinctual self and Chochmah.

☾

ᛦ
ELEMENT

*T*HERE ARE FOUR PRIMARY ELEMENTS, OR FUNDAMENTAL building blocks of creation: fire, air, water and earth. Each month is associated with one of these four elements. However, it is important to note that while manifesting physically, these elements are also meant to be understood in a much more metaphysical sense as well, as they represent numerous properties, qualities, and correspondences.*

---

* For a more in-depth exploration of these elements and their relationship to the Hebrew calendar, please see the introductory volume of this series: *The Spiral of Time: Unraveling the Yearly Cycle*.

Earth is the element associated with the month of Elul. Earth is cold and dry, representing a spiritual coldness and dryness, expressed through an absence of any Torah-based or even rabbinic holidays. Elul is a month of hard personal work. As Chassidus teaches, during Elul: The King (Hashem) is in the Field [along with us]. On one hand, this corresponds to the curse of Adam, when he was exiled from the Garden of Eden: "The Earth is cursed on account of you. Only through hard toil shall you receive sustenance from it all the days of your life" (*Bereishis*, 3:17). Our life and the past year is the field, our Teshuvah is the toil. On the other hand, although this month doesn't have any Holidays, every day of Elul is an opportune time to connect with Divinity. Since the King is 'in the field,' He is more readily accessible to all; we only need to approach the King and make our requests. The earthy quality of this month alludes to our calling to become more grounded, meaning to experience our essential closeness to Hashem in our day-to-day life, present 'in the field,' as it were.

☾

❧
TORAH PORTIONS

O VER THE COURSE OF A MONTH, 4-5 WEEKLY TORAH POR-
TIONS are read by the community. These individual portions can be combined and viewed as a single unit based
on the particular month in which they are most commonly read.
Indeed one finds, when viewing the *Parshas* through this calendrical lens, that an astounding array of thematic elements consistent
with the spiritual energy of the month are revealed.

Fittingly, the Torah portions we read during Elul, from Shoftim
through Nitzavim, teach us about Teshuvah (*Kedushas HaYehudi*, Elul),
healthy self-judgment, and self-improvement.

The portion of Shoftim begins: "You shall set up judges and law enforcement officials for yourself in all your gates (in the cities) that Hashem your God is giving you, for your tribes; and they shall judge the people (with) righteous judgment" (*Devarim*, 16:18). The specific instruction is to set up judges and law enforcement "for yourself." The body is a temple, a house for the soul, to be protected and guarded from dangerous and destructive influences. We have been given natural biological 'gates' to protect ourselves, such as eyelids to protect our vision, lips and teeth to protect our ingestion and speech, earlobes to allow us to filter the sounds that reach us, and nostrils to close against unwanted scents. It is up to us to devise a system of judgment and law enforcement 'for ourselves;' to use these naturally provided 'gates' to guard our senses from harmful input (*Shach*, ibid). The verse also specifies "righteous judgment," alluding to the wholesome, joyful way we are to scrutinize our lives during this month.

Parshas Ki Teitzei begins: "If you go out to battle 'above' your enemies, and Hashem your G-d delivers them into your hands..." (*Devarim*, 21:10). Spiritually, this refers to the battle with our own *Yetzer Hara* / inclination toward negative states, words, and actions. The verse is telling us, 'Know that you are essentially *above* your internal enemies, and you can and will be victorious!' During this month of Teshuvah, we should call forth the part of us deep within, that which is 'above' struggle.

Parshas Ki Savo contains the *Tochecha* / the energies of rebuke that can manifest in our lives if we stray from our spiritual path. It also contains the blessings and states of fulfillment we will experience if we serve Hashem with joy. Getting clear on this relationship of cause and effect can motivate us to do Teshuvah even more diligently during the second half of Elul.

Parshas Nitzavim: the word *Nitzavim* means 'standing strong and upright,' reminding us that we can reclaim our full spiritual stature during this month of hard spiritual work. The source-teaching of Teshuvah is also found in this Torah reading: "For this Mitzvah that I commanded you today, it is not hidden from you and it is not distant" (*Devarim*, 30:11). According to Ramban, "this Mitzvah" refers to Teshuvah, and "today" is its most important element. Even in the last week of Elul, we should do Teshuvah 'today' — each day must be approached as if we are starting anew (*Sifri*, on the verse). Since every moment is literally a new creation never seen before, you can always start over, even right now!

ꙮ
SEASON OF THE YEAR

*T*HE SEASONAL QUALITIES OF EACH MONTH ARE INTRI-
CATELY related with the spiritual qualities of that time
of year. When daylight lasts for longer or shorter periods,
different kinds of spiritual light are being revealed on a subtle level
as well. The physical experiences of spring are external expressions
of an internal reality emanating during that season, such as the
vital pulse of new life and growth. All dark and dank months reflect an energy of corresponding spiritual 'coldness,' stimulating us
to seek warmth. People tend to keep to themselves when winter
begins and are more outgoing when summer starts. All of these
psycho-physical weather patterns reflect deeper spiritual truths, as
the mind-body complex is a reflection of the metaphysical qualities
of the soul and spiritual realm.

The subtle changes in the weather during the month of Elul can bring us a new energy and vitality. While it can still get hot at the end of the summer, there are now cooler days as well. Summer vacations are ending; some people move back to their winter homes, and students are starting school. There is a very strong sense of endings, and also a strong desire to start afresh. This psycho-seasonal shift of energy stimulates us to look inward and 'inhale' the past year, gather all of it into our consciousness, and take spiritual stock in preparation for the High Holidays.

In such transitional moments there is a more pronounced longing to be authentic and not lose our way in life. In Elul (much like in Adar), we yearn to return to our true nature, our pure soul-essence, to reclaim our inner *Besulah* or 'virginal purity.' It is important to keep in mind that our drive toward self-evaluation and Teshuvah comes from a deep love and attraction to who we really are. It is certainly not meant to be a path of frustration and self-rejection.

Cosmically, Elul is a time of 'silence' that comes before the creation of the World on Rosh Hashanah, the silence before the sounding of the Shofar. The Shofar blast is considered the first sound of the year — the initiatory vibration that gives birth to the next cycle of creation, the first cry of a newborn. The act of creation occurs through sound: "And Hashem *said,* 'Let there be light,' and there was light." The Divine Speech sends into motion every facet of created reality. Elul is a time dedicated to the silence before sound. Our quiet introspection, self-analysis and spiritual work, gives rise to the 'birthing cries' of the new year, the new world, and our new lives.

Incessant noise is so much a part of our daily life that we have seemingly become dependent on it for our wellbeing. Many derive a sense of being alive from talking and from plugging themselves into constant audio stimulation. They feel uncomfortably empty in silence. There is a compulsion to break any silence and to talk, to play music, or even just mentally to sing or hum or chatter to oneself.

Underneath this urgency for noise is a terrible fear of being alone with ourselves and perhaps having a genuine self-encounter. Yet, it is only in being silent that we can get to know and love who we are. If we become comfortable with ourselves in silence, then, when we do need to speak we can do so with mindfulness and wisdom.

Silence opens up a space for soul-searching and inner-excavation. Soul-searching is not merely looking at the 'bad' or negative things we have done, or the positive things we never got around to achieving. If you focus only on 'how bad you are,' or what you failed at, or could not change, then you will most likely continue reenacting those negative behaviors, as your focus will only serve to reinforce their fundamental role in your story and identity.

Elul is more about finding and focusing on the blessings, wisdom and goodness in your life and past year. While we do need to recognize and separate from what is not working for us, we are really looking at ourselves and our behaviors in order to find the inner Yud, the inner *Besulah* within them. This does not mean that we are only looking on the revealed positive aspects of our past year and ignoring our shortcomings; it means that when we acknowledge the places in our lives that we can improve or the ways we missed the mark, we do so with the intention of finding the positive take-away from such self-reflection, not merely to beat ourselves up and feel guilty.

If you believe that you are blessed and your life is a blessing, then you will be blessed and you will be a blessing. In Elul, we have to delve within until we find that inner innocence, that point of purity, that baseline of blessing, and that world of wisdom that we all have at our core. Through that discovery and reconnection we can empower ourselves to grow and become even better partners, parents, and protagonists for positive change in the coming year.

As Elul is a time of cosmic silence, there are Kabbalistic and Musar customs to practice *Ta'anis Dibbur* / fasting from speech throughout the entire month of Elul. If this practice is too difficult or impossible, you can still benefit from a miniature form of it every day. Before you go to sleep, give yourself a period of time to practice Ta'anis Dibbur. For example, at a particular time each night do not speak for at least 15 minutes and turn inward towards self-reflection. After some practice, you might extend this to an hour. The amount of time should challenge you, but it should not be oppressive to you, much less to others.

☾

༃

THE HOLIDAYS
OF THE MONTH

"**F**OR EVERYTHING THERE IS AN APPOINTED TIME" (*Koheles,* 3:1). In other words, everything happens according to Divine timing (Rebbe RaYatz, *Sefer haMa'amorim,* tof-shin-aleph, p. 59). Our Sages tell us that when we left Egypt, it was the appointed time for such liberation. This means not only that it occurred in the historically appropriate time, but also at the right time of year — the season best suited for this expression of Redemption (*Mechilta deRabbi Yishmael,* Bo, 16, on the verse in Tehillim, 68:7. *Rashi,* Sotah, 2a). This is the same principle behind every *Yom Tov*; the narrative and observance of each celebration or fast reflects and refracts the light of the natural world through a spiritual lens.

Furthermore, in the months that contain a *Yom Tov* / holiday, that Yom Tov embodies and encapsulates the energy of the entire month in condensed form. In a month that does not have a major holiday, that absence is also an expression of the unique energy of the month.

There are no actual Holidays in Elul, yet this month comprises the bulk of what is termed the *Yemei Ratzon* / Days of Divine Desire and Goodwill (*Tana D'vei Eliyahu* Zuta, 4. *Ma'te Ephrayim*, Siman 581:1). This is the final period of 40 days when Moshe was alone on the Mountain, obtaining forgiveness for the People following the episode of the Golden Calf and the smashing of the first *Luchos* / Tablets. Moshe went up the mountain for the final time on Rosh Chodesh Elul and came down 40 days later on Yom Kippur with the second Luchos. Moshe implored and Hashem forgave the incident of the Golden Calf in this period, and on Yom Kippur the atonement was fully revealed.

Because of this, Elul is a time for us to focus on forgiving ourselves, our family, our community, and every individual in our lives. Towards this end, it helps to write a journal during this time, detailing and reflecting on the events of the past year, considering who we need to forgive or ask forgiveness from, and meditating on who we want to be in the coming year. When we put all these thoughts on paper, it is easier to see the bigger picture and envision what we want to manifest in the coming year.

To help inspire this act of self-inventory and process of change, we blow the *Shofar* / ram's horn every day from the first day of Elul through the day preceding the eve of Rosh Hashanah. Why? As we said, on the first of Elul Moshe ascended Mount Sinai for the third time, following the breaking of the first Luchos. This time his ascent was accompanied by the sound of the Shofar, which was blown throughout the camps in the Desert. The Shofar blasts marked the day that Moshe ascended the mountain, so the people would not repeat the same mistake of miscalculating the date of his return (the very mistake which led to the construction of the Golden Calf). In remembrance of this daily counting during this period, we too blow the Shofar during Elul (*Magen Avraham*, Orach Chayim, Siman 581:2. Quoting the *Tur*, ad loc. *Da'as Zekeinim*, Devarim, 10:10). However, according to some commentators, if it were for this reason alone, it would suffice to simply blow the Shofar on the first day of Elul (*Pirkei D'Rebbe Eliezer*, 46. See *Bach*, ibid.). Why then do most people have the custom to blow the Shofar throughout the entire month?* The answer is that the Shofar is intimately related to Teshuvah and inner awakening. It is our daily spiritual alarm clock to WAKE UP!

The piercing sound of the Shofar rouses the heart and awakens a person to the awesomeness of Hashem's Presence and to the charge of their own life (*Beis Yoseph*, ibid). As the Prophet Amos (3:6) says, "Could the Shofar be blown in the city, and the nation not tremble?"**

---

* According to the Rokeach, they blew the Shofar in the Midbar every day of the 40 days: *Sefer Rokeach*, 207. See also *haManhig*, Hilchos Rosh Hashanah, 24.

** "We have learned in *Pirkei D'Rebbe Eliezer*, on Rosh Chodesh Elul Hashem told Moshe, 'ascend to me on the mountain,' for it was then that he went to receive the second Luchos. And it was then they blew a Shofar in the camp, so everyone should know that Moshe went up the mountain, so that they should not make the same mistake and end up serving idols. As last time Moshe ascended

Each day in *Shul* / synagogue we blow the Shofar to sensitize ourselves to feel the urgency of awakening and reorienting our life in this very moment. The Days of Awe are imminent.

In the words of Rabbeinu Yonah, in this time period "a person shall tremble and be in awe from the dread of judgment" (*Sefer haY-irah*, towards the end). This "awe" is not the shallow fear of being judged, nor the fear of punishment. It is the awesome urgency of the need to take up full responsibility for our lives and for our world. Hashem's judgment is meant to inspire us to say to ourselves, "Wow, this little 'me' is invested with such power and purpose! My actions actually matter!" How can we live with this powerful awareness and not be overwhelmed? We must rely on Teshuvah, the process of constantly refining our character. The sense of awe in approaching Rosh Hashanah arouses a palpable desire for Teshuvah, as we want to be able see and show ourselves in full transparency without shame.

---

the mountain, the people miscalculated his return date, and when he did not show up on the mistaken date, they created the Golden Calf. Therefore our sages instituted that we too shall blow the Shofar on Rosh Chodesh Elul every year. And not only the first day, but also the entire month, in order to warn the people to do Teshuvah, as the verse says: 'Could the Shofar be blown in the city, and the nation not tremble?' And we also blow the Shofar during Elul to confuse the Satan" (Tur, *Orach Chayim*, 581). In other words, there is the Shofar blowing for Rosh Chodesh specifically, as a reminder of the Shofar that was blown in the desert, and there is the Shofar blowing throughout the entire month of Elul, which is connected to inspiring Teshuvah (and to confuse the Satan). The Rosh Chodesh Shofar blowing was to ensure that they do not 'sin' again; the Shofar blowing throughout the month is actually to awaken one to Teshuvah.

Thus, even if a person prays in solitude, there is a major opinion that he should still blow the Shofar by himself. In other words, the Shofar is not just a Mitzvah of the *Klal* / community, but also of each person individually, each *Perat*.*

The visceral sound of the Shofar causes us to tremble and consider that perhaps we have been sleeping all this time. Perhaps we have been passively riding through life on autopilot and were never really awake to the miracles of life, to its deeper purpose and meaning, or to our own true worth and potential. As harsh as it may sound, perhaps we are just 'alive' because we have not been killed in an accident. Perhaps we are living like robots, perhaps we have never truly exercised our free choice, and have only been living in reaction to our surroundings like puppets. When we hear the Shofar we arouse a healthy anxiety that if we are not careful we might just sleep through the better part of our life.

If we are living semi-consciously, we are not actively connected to our deeper self, nor to the Creator of the World. If we are spiritually or mentally asleep, we may feel free of worry or anxiety or a need to act, but we are really only just suppressing our intrinsic soul-knowledge.

---

* There is an argument whether or not the shofar-blowing in Elul is a 'responsibility of the *tzibur*' only. The first time a shofar was blown — when Moshe went up to Mount Sinai — it was blown in the Camp. Is hearing the shofar then the responsibility of an individual who is praying alone? Rabbi Tzvi Pesach Frank and the *Shu't Siach Yitzchak*, (264) says, we should blow whether or not we are in a congregation. The *Tzitz Eliezer* (Vol 12, Siman 48) says we only need to blow if we are praying with a congregation. The accepted custom is that if a person is praying alone, the shofar should still be blown.

Once we are aroused from such slumber, our spiritual instincts come alive again, and we shudder with the realization that something has been amiss.

To begin to do Teshuvah, we first need to wake up. The shrill shriek of the Shofar wakes us up, and stokes our desire to return to conscious, mindful, meaningful life in harmony with our higher purpose.

During our journeys in the Desert, the war with Sichon and Og ended in Elul. The time after this great war was revealed as a time of Divine *Ratzon* / will and desire. This is why, during this month, Moshe prayed 515 times to enter the Holy Land. Elul is a time of Divine goodwill and desire, and thus it is a month when prayers are readily accepted on High.*

☾

---

*In addition to the blowing of the Shofar each day (besides Shabbos) and reciting Chap 27 of Tehilim (and Selichos), the Baal Shem Tov instituted the custom of reciting three additional chapters of Tehilim each day, from the first of Elul until Yom Kippur. (On Yom Kippur the remaining 36 chapters are recited). Elul is also an appropriate time to have one's Tefillin and Mezuzos checked.

The Divine Desire to Create the World

Even before the episode of the golden calf, Elul was considered a time of *Cheshek* / Divine Desire. The earliest example of this is that Elul is the 'time' when Hashem felt the initial urge to create the world.*

There is a well-known debate between our sages about when, exactly, the creation of the human being occurred. Rabbi Eliezer is of the opinion that the creation of humanity was on the first day of the month of Tishrei, Rosh Hashanah. Rabbi Yehoshua, however, argues that it was the first day of the month of Nisan (*Rosh Hashanah*, 11a). The Arizal (*Sha'ar HaKavanos*, Rosh Hashanah, Derush 1), reconciles these opinions saying that the viable 'pregnancy' of the world began in Tishrei and the actual 'birth' occurred in the month of Nisan. Similarly, during the fall and winter months between Tishrei and Nisan, the life-force of the natural world is dormant and hidden, as in pregnancy. The actual birth and flowering of the life-force then reveals itself in Nisan, the spring.

On Rosh Hashanah we declare, "*HaYom Haras Olam* / Today a world is born." In this context, 'born' actually means 'in pregnancy' as *Haras* comes from the word *Hirayon* / pregnant.

---

* Even though this occurred before time itself was created, we can understand Elul as a symbol of a timeless time prior to the creation of the world. "Hashem felt a Cheshek" is similarly symbolic language.

Therefore, an alternative translation of *HaYom Haras Olam* could be: 'Today, on Rosh Hashanah, the world is confirmed as a viable embryo; we can joyfully expect the actual birth six months from now, in the month of Nisan!'(See *Pri Eitz Chayim*, Shar HaShofar, 5. *Ben Yehoyada*, Rosh Hashanah, 10b).

The above reconciliation of the sages' debate is reminiscent of a commentary from Tosefos (*Rosh Hashanah*, 27a), which explains that the thought of creating humanity 'entered the Creator's mind' in Tishrei, whereas the actual creation took place six months later in Nisan. According to this view, on Rosh Hashanah the world as well as human beings exist as a thought within the mind of the Creator, in the realm of *Beriah*. This is similar to a fetus existing within the womb of the mother. In both cases, only later is the creation actually born into the tangible realm of *Asiyah* / action.

Let's extend the metaphor of conception a little deeper. Before conception there is intimacy, and before intimacy there is a strong desire to be intimate, a craving to unite. This desire to create would have arisen prior to Tishrei, during Elul. In Elul, the Creator 'imagined' creating an 'other' entity, and fantasized, as it were, what such a creation would look like. Hashem thus imagined the wonderful spiritual work that the righteous people of the future world would do (*Medrash Rabbah*, Bereishis 8:7), and this is what awakened the strong desire to conceive a world.

Since the Divine Cheshek of the Creator for creation resonates eternally within the month of Elul, we are also aroused with a Cheshek for Hashem during this time. This is one reason why we meditate in Elul on the verse *Ani leDodi* / I am my Beloved's.

Elul is therefore the time of the *Yetziras haVelad* / the formation of the fetus of the world. According to Halachah, the formation of an embryo into a viable fetus takes 40 days from conception. If the date of the 'creation' of humanity is Rosh Hashanah, the first day of the creation of the world is six days prior, on the 25th of Elul. If we view this date as not the actual creation, but the first sign of the viable formation of the fetus, then we can count back 40 days to conception. Forty days before the 25th of Elul is in fact Tu b'Av, the day of Divine love which conceived the world. Thus the entire period of Elul is a time of the Yetziras haVelad, and the 25th of Elul is when our worldly reality has become a halachic *Ibur* / pregnancy.

It takes 40 days to form a *Beriah chadashah* / new creation, to arrive at or determine a new status of being. Similarly, after immersing in a Mikvah that contains 40 *Sa'ah* of water, a person emerges as a Beriah Chadashah (Arizal, *Sha'ar haLikutim*, Tehilim, 51 on the Pasuk *Lev Tahor*). That is, fully immersing in a Mikvah is like re-entering the womb and a pre-birth state, thus when one emerges one becomes as a newborn (*Sefer haChinuch*, Mitzvah 173). From this we can learn that the 40 days between Elul and Yom Kippur are a kind of Mikvah-in-time.

In 40 days there are 960 hours, just as there are 960 *Lugin* in 40 *Sa'ah* of water. This fact alludes to the great importance of every hour of Elul in engaging with our self-formation (our own *Yetziras haVelad*) and rebirth (*Devash l'Phi*, Aleph, 12). This is the real Avodah of Elul, to imagine ourselves the way we want to be, and to re-form ourselves according to that vision.

A beautiful way to visualize this process is to remember that Elul is the letter Yud. Yud is the top of every letter in the Aleph-Beis, and from the Yud the body of the letter extends downward and outward. In this way, Yud, which is shaped like a point or a drop, is the seminal potential of every expression. During the month of *Yetziras haVelad*, we are actively forming ourselves and creating the conditions for the inception of our future actualization during the coming year.

"Everything is לדעתן נבראו /created according to its own permission" (*Rosh Hashanah,* 11a. *Rashi,* לדעתם). On some deep level, our experience is up to us; we have the choice as to how we ourselves, and our new year, will be formed and created. On Rosh Hashanah we have already become an *Ibur,* a formed fetus, and our *Yetzirah /* formation is already confirmed. Therefore it is in Elul that we need to demonstrate to ourselves and to Hashem what our intention and 'permission' really is. Do we permit Hashem to recreate us? Do we really feel that we deserve to be formed into a viable 'fetus'? Do we recognize and believe in the deeper importance of our own existence? Can we produce evidence of our commitment to living and developing and to being reborn? Can we justify our life in the coming year? Hashem is asking us precisely these existential questions in Elul, and our answers allow us to become co-creators in our own (re)formation.

Our sages (Yerushalmi, *Rosh Hashanah,* 4:8) note that with regard to all the offerings in the Beis HaMikdash the Torah says, "and you shall offer," whereas with the offerings of Rosh Hashanah, the Torah says, "and you shall make." Thus we are not 'offering' but 'making' ourselves in this process of approaching Rosh Hashanah; we need to form our being in Elul as if from an embryonic state. Afterward, Hashem tells us, "Since you have passed before Me in judgment on

Rosh Hashanah, and you have emerged whole, I do consider you as a *Beriah chadashah*" (ibid., Rabbi Yossi). It is very important to emphasize this process of Yetziras haVelad in relation to our meditation and action during Elul. It is, in fact, the very essence of the *Avodah* / spiritual work for this month.

The Thirteen Attributes of Mercy & the 'King in the Field'

Throughout the month of Elul, the Thirteen Attributes of Divine Compassion are openly revealed (*Pri Eitz Chayim*, Sha'ar Rosh Hashanah. *Mishnas Chasidim*, Meseches Elul, 1:3). * The *Gematria* / numerical value of the word Elul, in *Mispar Katan* / small numbers, is 13: Aleph=1, Lamed=3, Vav=6, Lamed=3. In *Mispar Katan*, the numerical value of each letter is reduced to its decimal value; i.e., 30 becomes 3. The value 13 is also the Gematria of the word *Ahavah* / Love as well as the word *Echad* / One. All of these hints point to the fact that Elul is a time of great Divine love, compassion, and desire to create on the level of *Penimiyus haOlam* / the inner dimension of the world. Thus, the month of Elul vibrates with the loving desire of a mother for her unborn child, still in formation.

---

* Just the mere act of reciting the 13 Attributes with proper Kavanah draws down its power (*Rabbeinu Bachya*, Ki Tisa. *Sha'ar haFla'ah*, see *Bnei Yissachar*, Elul, 2:4). The Alshich and many other sources write that we need to embody these qualities if they are to have an effect *Alshich*, Bamidbar, 14:20. *Reishis Chochmah*, Sha'ar haAnava 1.

אני לדודי ודודי לי / *Ani leDodi veDodi Li...* / I am to my Beloved and my Beloved is to me [Who grazes among the roses] (*Shir haShirim*, 6:3). The first letters of these four words form an acronym that spells *Elul*. "Roses" refers to the Thirteen Attributes of Mercy, as the Zohar teaches (1, 1a), "Just as there are thirteen petals on a rose, so the People of Israel are surrounded on all sides by the Thirteen Attributes of Mercy" (Alter Rebbe, *Siddur Im Dach*, Sha'ar Elul).

Elul is a time of *Rachamim* / Divine compassion alone; there is no judgment, just *Rachamim* (*Sh'ut Node b'Yehudah*, Orach Chayim, 32). It is also a time when the cosmic Divine desire to create is aroused, which is rooted in an even deeper desire to share and to give. Thus, as it says so beautifully in the Psalms, "The world shall be built with Chesed" (*Tehilim*, 89:3). This foundation of Creation was first revealed in Elul, and is forever the spiritual quality of this month.

In fact, the revealing of the Thirteen Attributes that occurred during this month, as recorded in the Torah, secures blessings for the body and all of our material needs including physical abundance, life, and health (The Thirteen Attributes drawn from *Micha* 7:18-20, on the other hand, are blessings for spiritual life. See *Siddur Im Dach*, Sha'ar Elul*).

---

* The word אלול, when divided in two, spells the words לא / not, and לו / to him. The verse (*Yeshayahu*, 63:9) is written as, "בכל-צרתם לא צר / In all their troubles, He is לא / not troubled," whereas it is read as "בכל צרתם לו צר / In all their troubles, לו / He is troubled." There is a level of Transcendence such that our actions below have no effect on High, this is לא, with an Aleph, the totally impenetrable level of Keser. And there is a level of Divine Immanence, where our actions do have an effect on high, this is לו with a Vav, the relatable and relational realm of the Six Lower Sefiros. In Elul, there is a revealing of the 13 Transcendent Attributes of Keser into the lower realms of our experience, and thus there is a unique aspect of Divine forgiveness for our misdirected actions available during this time. Tzemach Tzedek, *Ohr Torah*, Re'eh.

This revelation of Divine Mercy begins on the First of Elul and climaxes with the *Ne'ilah* / culminating prayers of Yom Kippur, during which the Thirteen Attributes are completely manifest.

As we said, there are no official Holidays in the month of Elul. And yet Elul makes up the bulk of the *Yemei Ratzon* / Days of Divine Desire and Goodwill, when Moshe was alone on the Mountain, obtaining forgiveness for the People following the sin of the golden calf. These days are thus characterized by an exceptional level of intimacy and transparency between the human and Divine realms.

Such an exalted revelation as the Thirteen Attributes can normally only occur during elevated holidays, when 'the King is in the Palace,' His rightful place of Righteous Power. At those times, we are in a state of pure *being*. Above and beyond the constant *doing* that fills and fuels the mundane world. In order for us to sense the presence of such an exalted revelation we usually need to transcend our normal state, such as by refraining from work and unplugging from our electronic devices. Yet Elul is not comprised of holidays at all, but of mundane days, when we must actively attend to our spiritual state even while we go about our daily tasks. Elul is thus a reality of *being* that paradoxically includes *doing*. This is much like Purim, when the highest spiritual reality is revealed, yet, we are free to perform worldly and mundane tasks as needed. In fact, Elul and Purim both represent the highest revelation of G-dliness; when the Divine is welcomed into and revealed within the mundane world. This is what is ultimately meant by *Hashem Echad* / G-d is One.

Rabbi Schneur Zalman of Liadi, affectionately known as the *Alter* / old Rebbe, illustrates this characteristic of Elul with a parable (*Likutei Torah*, Parshas Re'eh): In ancient times, if a subject desired to make a request of the king, he had to go through many channels, protocols and bureaucracies, until he could finally approach the king. Before the ministers presented him before the king, he was taught all the proper ways of formally addressing him, how to bow, when to speak and when not to speak. Finally, once he attained the king's presence, he had merely a few short moments to express himself.

At certain times, however, the king would travel outside the city. When he was traveling through the fields surrounding his palace, anyone who desired to meet the king could easily approach without the artificial intervention of protocol and bureaucracy.

Similarly, says the Alter Rebbe, during the month of Tishrei, the Divine King is in his Heavenly court of judgment within His transcendent palace. In Elul, however, the King is passing through the fields where common people live — a place of mundane work and personal concerns. Therefore, anyone who desires to approach Hashem with their needs during this month may do so. The King Himself is also more relaxed, as it were, and is more apt to show a smiling and friendly face to all who approach him at this time.

In this way, Elul is paradoxically mundane and transcendent all at once. This is the month of the highest revelation, as the Supreme King is intimately present every moment, and yet, Elul is composed of regular, unremarkable days, devoid of any special holidays or observances. This paradox is possible because Elul is intimately connected with the holiness and revelation of Tishrei, the subsequent month that is literally filled with holidays. In a sense, the two months are a single unit. This dynamic is similar to the month of Adar, the mundane month of Purim, which precedes Nisan, the holy month of Pesach. In Adar, transcendence and immanence also paradoxically intermingle, revealing something greater: the expansive and inclusive *Kedusha* / holiness of the King Himself revealed within the *Chol* / emptiness or mundane weekday reality.

The Purpose of a King

Let us go a little deeper into this metaphor of a king, and in particular, a "king [who is] in the field," accessible, approachable, and wants to show his subjects a kind, loving face.

What is the deeper purpose of an earthly king? In ancient Israel, the people of Israel were ruled by kings for many centuries. Why was there a need for a king, and why is there apparently a Mitzvah to establish a king? If it was just to maintain law and order, for that purpose, there were already appointed judges and enforcers specifically for this task (*Devarim* 16:18). And if it was just to decide whether or not to go to war, a king would in any case need the permission of the *Sanhedrin* / High Court; certainly when it came to voluntary wars. Additionally, there were appointed generals for battle as well — so why a king?

In truth there is an argument regarding whether or not it is a Mitzvah to anoint a king; perhaps kingship was merely a Divine concession to the psycho-political desires and anxieties of the people who were not ready for real autonomy as Hashem initially intended (*Sanhedrin*, 20b). Yet, the Rambam (*Hilchos Melachim*) rules that there is in fact a Mitzvah to anoint a king. Especially if we accept the Rambam's position, we need to seriously inquire into the role and purpose of a king.

When the Torah describes the anointing of kings it says, "You shall surely set over yourself a king" (*Devarim*, 17:15). Our sages teach that this vertical language implies that "The awe of the king must be upon you" (*Sanhedrin*, 22a). As a consequence, the king must always be respected. A king cannot forego his honor (*Kesuvos*, 17a). By contrast, if a parent wants to forego his or her honor, that is their right. For example, a parent may tell his child, "According to Torah law you are not allowed to sit in my designated seat at the table, and furthermore, there is a Mitzvah to respect and honor your parents. On the other hand, I don't mind; you can sit in my place." According to Halachah, the child may then sit in the parent's seat. However, even if he wanted to, a king is prohibited from making such a concession or gesture.

Why can a father or mother forgo their honor, even though the Torah teaches, "One shall fear his father and mother," whereas a king cannot forgo his honor? What is the essential distinction (Mahari Perlo, *Sefer Hamitzvos Rasag*, 3, p. 119)? Various answers are offered, such as, the king's honor is not for the king himself, but rather for the institution of kingship. Another simple answer is, a king can only rule to the extent that he instills *Yirah* / awe and motivational fear. Yirah is therefore a king's definition, his *Metziyus* / his very existence. If a king forgives a breach of his honor, he is no longer a 'king.' He might be considered another kind of leader or public servant, but he no longer has the image and effect of an absolute ruler, and thereby no longer qualifies within the classification of king. This is unlike parents who can still be parents if they dismiss the idea of instilling awe in their children. The king and his power to create incentivized anxiety are inseparable.

Therefore, appointing and accepting a King over Klal Yisrael is meant to bestow the quality of holy awe upon us. This Mitzvah awakened within us a more relatable sense of the infinite majesty, awesomeness, grandeur, and power of the King of Kings. The almost superhuman presence of a worldly king inspires us to live with a constant sense of awe and amazement in the presence of a Supernal Other. It puts us in touch through analogy with the Ultimate Power of the Universe, and the glory which attracts us and simultaneously causes us to step back in trepidation. This aspect of the Divine is referred to as the Mysterium Tremendum. On the one hand we feel a compulsive urge to be in a relationship with a transcendent Other, and on the other hand we feel humbled and miniscule in such an infinite Presence. The purpose of the earthly king is thus to serve as a conduit of awe, not necessarily awe for the person himself (which is idolatrous), but rather for the institution of kingship itself, and all that it represents. Then, by association, we can elevate our awe toward the true King of Kings. The earthly king is therefore a means, not an end in himself. This fact is unfortunately often forgotten and abused by the common people or their appointed ruler, who pervert the essential purpose of this arrangement, and seek to manipulate it for personal gain and aggrandizement. This is quite literally the very definition of idol worship, and yet it is all too common, even today.

Either way, a true and Torah-aligned king serves as a conduit for higher Yirah. In the traditional language of Kabbalah and Chassidus, the objective of this royal Yirah is *Bitul* / humble nullification of the separate 'I' in the presence of the Omnipresent (*Derech Mitzvosecha*, "Mitzvas Minui Melech").

Hashem has an 'aspect' of immanence and an 'aspect' of transcendence. Of course, there is only one Hashem, however, the One can be experienced in many aspects or reflections. Related to the immanent aspect of Hashem we can feel close; there is a palpable 'personal' relationship of *Ahavah* / love. Regarding the transcendent aspect of Hashem, there is *Yirah*, trepidation, reverence and awe.

The Creator's generative and sustaining Light manifests as the transcendent *Ohr Sovev Kol Almin* / light that surrounds all worlds, and simultaneously as the imminent *Ohr Memaleh Kol Almin* / light that fills all creation. *Sovev* is the light that 'encompasses' and transcends creation, inspiring reverence and trembling — even a kind of spiritual terror when one beholds the ultimate mystery of the Majestic One whose existence eclipses Creation. There is an inevitable collapse of ego in this perception of the indescribable majesty of the King of Kings. *Memaleh* is the light that fills the universe, permeating all creation, allowing us to love the Creator and feel at home in the world. We need both of these lights and experiences. Engaging specifically with the metaphor of the 'King' — representing honor, fear, awe, majesty, power, transcendence — opens us up and helps us to experience a level of *Sovev* and a corresponding type of *Bitul*.

In other words, if we see someone or something as holding the power of life or death, we become responsive and alert; it is clear to us that our every act in their presence or purview has great consequence. Assuming it is a benevolent ruler, we also rush to harmonize ourselves with his or her will, and heed their advice and decrees. We do not stop to second-guess their seriousness or challenge their reasoning. Hashem is *haMelech haTov* / the All benevolent King. His advice and decrees are the Mitzvos. He wants us to choose life and "live by them." This requires us to get out of our own way, so to speak, and live with a healthy sense of *Bitul.* Our Creator wants us to be full of Divine wisdom (Torah) instead of the false, self-serving wisdom of *Yeshus* / ego. Hashem knows this is a matter of life or death for us. Without investing in a relationship with the Supreme King, we are indeed in danger of following the deceptive and ultimately lethal advice of His lesser ministers or the selfish ego.

The Smiling King

As we are approaching the awesome moment of Creation, Rosh Hashanah, there is a renewed Divine desire to create and sustain Creation. Thus we sense more vividly the awesome presence of the Omnipotent King, as this transcendent, all-powerful aspect of Hashem seeks to express itself anew. Yet, according to the beautiful parable of the Alter Rebbe: "In Elul, the King is smiling and showing a pleasant face to all." This is therefore also a time, as the Arizal teaches, when the Thirteen Attributes of compassion are being revealed — a time of Divine grace. Elul is thus a time of both Creation and Compassion, of transcendence and immanence, of Yirah and Ahavah, of Elokim and the Four Letter Name. The King is simultaneously the Cosmic Creator, the Awesome Judge, and the Compassionate Friend, showing each one of us a 'face' of love and kindness. There is thus a strong sense of judgment and a corresponding need to 'justify' our existence, and yet, there is also a "pleasant," comforting awareness that the King is smiling at us (Although a king may not forgo his honor, as explained, this can refer to his honor in either the present or the future, however, it is perhaps possible that he may forgo his honor of the past. "כל המורד במלך ישראל יש למלך רשות להרגו /The king has the **right** to execute anyone who rebels against a king" (Rambam, *Hilchos Melachim*, 3:8). This can mean that he could or could not forgo on his honor. See also, *Yad Ramah*, Sanhedrin, 48b)). Despite the anxiety there is no reason to panic and run, rather we feel a personal invitation, and a magnetic desire to bask in the awesomeness and greatness of the King.

Bring to mind a great person or hero, one whom you have always wanted to meet, someone for whom you have a lot of respect, and almost awe. Maybe this is a person who lived many years ago, perhaps a great grandparent or a beloved historical figure such as a Chasidic luminary, or one of the Matriarchs or Patriarchs. Now, visualize that you are about to enter a room and meet this person and be in their presence. As you open the door, you see this person is smiling at you warmly and welcoming you by name. What do you feel? What are you moved to say or do? Do you ask a question, make a request, or perhaps simply bask in their presence?

In the presence of a great person you feel great. Many of us would just want to spend more time with them. The King, the Ultimate Source of all Greatness, is in the 'field,' our territory, throughout Elul. We are given the amazing privilege of being in the presence of the King whenever we desire. We just need to turn and face Him; this is *Teshuvah* / (re)turning. We are also given the requisite spiritual senses to perceive the King's presence wherever we go. All we want to do in this condition is be with the King, to be in the presence of *haGadol* / the Great One. Maybe we will ask for something and maybe not, but that is secondary, the ultimate pleasure is simply to bask in G-d's infinite Greatness.

One thing is for sure: in such a state of being aware and present with the Omnipotent King there is no room for pettiness, smallness or the persistence of petty issues or negative problems. Everything falls by the wayside. Your smallness disappears as you are lifted up into the limitless Heart of Greatness; in fact, you too become great. All you want to do is be your deepest self.

This is another reason why we blow the Shofar in Elul. It is through the blowing of the Shofar that we externalize our essence. We exhale our *Neshamah* / soul through this powerful *Neshimah* / outbreath. And as we exhale and express our deepest self into existence through the primal sound of the Shofar, all our smallness and pettiness evaporates in the prayerful reverberations.

A Time to Reorient Ourselves

Elul is the month in which the Omnipresent Creator's desire to be intimate with us, and for that reason to create us and to give us 'being,' is aroused. This, too, is why we may feel the desire to simply 'be' during this time — to be present, and to reveal our souls. Elul is thus a time to show up, to reorient and recreate our lives. This is the essence of Teshuvah.

Teshuvah is often about the details; 'I have done this or that, I have neglected this or that, I would like to fix such-and-such aspect of my character,' etc. In Elul, however, we need to take Teshu-vah to a deeper level and see the bigger picture. We need to think about our life as a whole, and whether or not we are orienting it towards Hashem. Are we living with the awareness of constantly being in the presence of the Omnipresent One? Are we living our life knowing that we are perpetually in the presence of the Ulti-mate Greatness? Are we truly engaging our gifts and greatness to the best of our abilities? These are the types of questions we must answer in Elul.

When we view Elul as the period of *Yetziras haVelad*, the cre-ation of a viable life, we can see that the Teshuvah of Elul tends to-wards questions of our very existence, of life as a whole. Then, when we engage in the practice of self-examination from this perspective, it is not so much about the details, but rather about returning to being deeply present with the King and Master of the world.

Is my basic orientation and fundamental desire to live with the awareness that I am always in the presence of the King? Without this basic, bigger picture view, we are just dealing in endless details and trying continually to fill-in the ever-widening gaps, the small pockets of emptiness in our lives.

If we get carried away with the details, doing one Mitzvah and then another, fixing one negative attribute then another, there can be no cohesion or internal connection across all our actions and choices. Our good actions are still good, but they may not be oc-curring within a holistic paradigm, and there will still remain an emptiness on the core level of life. Without an overarching theme to our lives, even our well-intentioned actions might lack a deliberate and unified trajectory. The bigger picture of our relationship to the King infuses our individual spiritual works with purpose, and connects the dots of our seemingly isolated experiences, mistakes and good deeds; forming a redemptive whole out of the myriad details of our lives.

Elul is about becoming aware of this bigger picture; there is a King and we are living in the King's presence. We are empowered to serve the King by creating a dwelling place for Him here, in this world. The rest is commentary.

Over the past several hundred years many communities have had a custom to recite chapter 27 of *Tehilim* / Psalms each day from the First of Elul through the Festival of Sukkos (*Siddur*, Alter Rebbe, Hilchos Keriyas Shema v'Tefilah). Within this chapter there is a most important verse. King David says, "אחת שאלתי/*Achas Sha'alti...* / One thing have I asked [of Hashem, and that will I seek, that I dwell in the house of Hashem all the days of my life]" (*Tehilim*, 27:4). Clearly, there are many things we need in life: good health, *Nachas* / delight in our children, financial stability, good relationships and so forth. There are also many things we need to support us in leading a spiritual life, such as peace of mind, clarity, perseverance, inspiration, and strength. But all these are really just details. The all-inclusive quest and the *Achas* / one and most important thing that we must seek is: "that I dwell in the house of Hashem all the days of my life." This is the essential goal, the big picture. In Elul, we are empowered to begin living with this true soul-desire and awareness as the centerpiece and cornerstone of our consciousness.

As we mentioned earlier, the 40 days from the first of Elul through Yom Kippur is considered a "Mikvah of time." These days are a veritable pool of purifying waters within the dimension of time. In general, a Mikvah is *meTaher* / purifying when a person immerses with every part of their body in the water, and then re-emerges. There is, however, a pertinent law concerning the water in a Mikvah: the water must be 'gathered' but must also be flowing in its natural state. When this is not the case, such as when water has been gathered in any bucket or tubing no matter the size, that 'impure' or unfit water can become 'pure' or fit for the Mikvah through *Hashakah* / touching or kissing (Mishnah, *Beitza*, 17b. *Pesachim*, 34b). In other words, if the unfit water is touching other waters in such a way that are fit for the Mikvah, the 'impure' water becomes 'pure.'

The deeper meaning of this is that all the individual details of one's life do need to be immersed within the holy, purifying waters of Teshuvah to become pure. But there is also a type of Teshuvah that occurs simply by *Hashakah* — 'touching' the awesome Divine King. By reorienting the water of our life as a whole to 'touch' the Pure Water of the King's Presence, our impure details become pure at once. This is the opposite of 'guilty by association,' in this case we become 'holy by association.' In Elul, we need to draw near to the King, in order to reach out and 'touch' his hand or sleeve; we thereby connect to His limitless essence.

Such contact would be almost too frightening to consider or suggest if it were not for the fact that the King, Who is in the field during this time, is also our Compassionate Father and Beloved Friend. Indeed, Teshuvah is only possible within a paradigm of Hashem as a loving Parent and we as a child. As mentioned, a king cannot forgo his honor and forgive our trespasses, yet a parent may. Accordingly, Hashem's warm smile of recognition during this time inspires within us a *Cheshek* / desire to immerse ourselves in the purifying 'waters' of His presence. We are thus drawn ever deeper into relationship with the Master of the universe.

On the other hand, knowing that there is a benevolent Monarch behind the seeming chaos of the universe helps us ingrain into our minds the empowering truth that our lives have meaning and purpose. This means that there is an important reason why we are each here. The metaphor of a King-subject relationship, as distinct from a Parent-child relationship, helps us understand that not only are we created by a loving Creator, but that we are charged with a specific mission. In this vast kingdom, each of us is entrusted with a unique mandate to fulfill on behalf of our Master, one that only we alone can achieve. The smiling Divine face in Elul gives us the strength to pursue our mission like a valiant warrior-poet. As a consequence, our lives vibrate with ever deeper levels of meaning from moment to moment. As we become an extension of the King's will, we are invested with the power to co-create ourselves and the very world we inhabit.

Once the bigger picture of this Divine relationship is secure in our consciousness, we have to demonstrate it in our daily life. The question is, how? The intellectual acknowledgements of this ultimate reality alone, and our place within it, do not seem to necessarily have the practical effects on life that we need in order to transform our lives. We may be inspired with a heightened awareness for a few hours, days or maybe even weeks, but eventually we tend to return to our old patterns of behavior. Therefore, if this illuminating realization is not put into practice in some way, we will likely just end up back in our old, petty labyrinth of self-centeredness.

So how do we use the higher wisdom and awareness that we gain in Elul to actually change our lives here on the ground? How do we ensure that which we know in our minds is translated into our hearts and expressed in our actions?

The Avodah / Work of Elul:
Rectifying our Subconscious Mind or Imagination

What we 'know,' theoretically, often has little effect on our actions. At times there can seem to be great inconsistencies between our intellectual understanding and our actual behavior. For example, a person could have a strong conviction that lying is harmful to himself and others; he could be an expert in the Torah's teachings about the prohibition against lying, and have years of psychological training in the reasons why people lie — all to no avail. How could his habit of lying remain untransformed after so much effort and investment? The answer lies in the fact that the conscious level of the mind is just one level. There are deeper levels of self, one of which we are calling the subconscious mind. The subconscious mind can, and often does, quite easily override our conscious knowledge, and thus often determines our behavior, seemingly 'against our will.'

When we find ourselves acting, speaking or thinking in ways that are contrary to our best intentions, it is often because there is a certain 'image' ingrained in our subconscious mind which is guiding us. This may be a deeply held self image, a subconscious identification pattern which may have been formed early in life, 'commanding' us to react from the context of that image. In this respect we can say that, in general, our conscious mind runs on ideas, whereas our unconscious mind speaks in the language of images. And as powerful as ideas are, images, especially when they are unconscious, are even deeper and more influential.

For instance: When we are in the presence of certain conditions or stimuli that stimulate or awaken our unconscious mind, this deep-seated self image surfaces and forces us to act, speak, and think contrary to our conscious control. Despite our conscious efforts, when the subconscious mind is triggered, such as when we are in a reactive mood, our actions, words, and thoughts will be a reflection of this deeper image, rather than an expression of our highest ideals.

This internal dynamic between ideas and images reveals a tension between our conscious, logical self and our deeper subconscious mind. In a certain sense, it is a tension between word and image, or between right-brain and left-brain modes of consciousness. The question is, if our subconscious mind exerts more influence on our behavior than our conscious mind, how do we transform our subconscious mind? How do we circumvent our logical, linear left-brain, and go deeper in order to uproot demoralizing fantasies rooted in unconscious conditioning? How do we take our understanding of the big picture, of living in the presence of Greatness and our own greatness, and ingrain it into our deepest instincts in a way that will empower us to transform our lives and relationships in a real, consistent way?

The answer is that we need to rewire our internal circuitry so that we can redirect our imagination and energies towards holiness and goodness, rather than being subsumed in the subconscious servitude of the tyrannical ego and our baser natures. This deep work requires more than new ideas about what is good or bad for us and the world, the radical shift we are suggesting requires us to actually transform our internal operating systems like intuition and instinct. To effect change on the structural and fundamental levels we are speaking of, we need to employ methods and mediums that speak in the language of our body, heart, and imagination, rather than just our brain. Music, rhythm and chant, for example, provide an excellent avenue into the subconscious mind. Additionally, the practice of repetitive simple actions is another way to develop a new 'second nature;' Elul, as we have discussed, is specifically connected with this strategy. Another powerful way to work on refining our subconscious mind is through the modality of visualization and imagery, as we will now discuss.

Creative Visualization and Re-programming the Subconscious

In the West we tend to focus on words and on intellectual, analytical approaches to self-transformation. Yet, much of who we are is informed not by the word but by the image. The Kabbalists teach that Redemption begins with redeeming our imagination, our power to dream and create holy imagery. Rabbi Tzadok of Lublin calls the early period of Jewish history until the destruction of the Second Beis HaMikdash / Temple the 'action' period. During this period we brought physical offerings as a way of transforming ourselves and our misdeeds. After the Temple period until today, our modes of Teshuvah are not as physically visceral. Self-transformation, since the destruction of the Second Temple, is now accomplished mainly through prayer and study — in other words, through text and language. We bring the "offerings of our mouths" (prayer) in place of material (i.e. animal or agricultural) offerings. In the coming Redemption, our 'offerings' will be even less physical than speech, in fact, we will only need to employ the 'garment' of 'thought' — meaning image and imagination — to express and effect our desired changes in ourselves and the world.

Exile is a condition of our alienation from the power of *Dimyon* / imagination. The Seforno writes that fantasy — meaning misdirected or false imagination — is the work of the *Nachash* / snake from the Garden of Eden. The Torah states that the snake was *Arum* (*Bereishis*, 3:1). Literally, the word *Arum* means sly, manipulative, and sneaky (*Berachos*, 17a, *Rashi*). The snake had, and represents, an over-active imagination that was trapped in a world of fantasy. This is a perversion of the essential power of imagination.

In order to manipulate her, the Snake thus sought to distort Chavah's imagination and instill within her a false, illusory, self-image. This clouded her true vision of reality, and, as a result, ours as well. The voice of the snake is a *Chitzoni* / external one, a voice that does not come from deep within, but rather from outside the self. By following this voice, Chavah and Adam were seduced into acting contrary to what they knew deep within to be true, and fell into the quicksand of fantasy and false imagination. They were lured by the snake's promise to be "like G-d" and began generating grandiose and arrogant visions of themselves.

This 'voice' of negative fantasy and shallowness is all around us, all the time. We are continually being bombarded with unhealthy images and manipulative messages from the popular culture and mass media, whether through explicit advertisements or subliminal imagery. These are messages or images that come into our purview from outside of us. After many years of being bombarded with such imagery and stimuli, these images accumulate in the storehouse of our subconscious mind. As a result, certain experiences can trigger this latent imagery and bring it up into our conscious awareness, like a belch. In this way we are led to act according to these 'voices' from outside of us, vying for our allegiance, often to our own detriment.

Amazingly, the words Nachash and Moshiach have the same numerical value (358). The Redemption of imagination requires transforming Nachash-consciousness, that shallow, external, skin-deep fantasy world, into Moshiach-consciousness, that faithful vision in a unified and perfected world of peace and holiness. False fantasy must therefore be converted into holy *Dimyon*. For if one cannot even imagine such a world, how can they dedicate their very lives to its promised manifestation?

But, considering the equivalence between the snake of fantasy and messianic redemption of imagination, it is important to seriously consider: What is the real difference between negative fantasy and positive Dimyon? Put simply, one chooses us, and the other we choose. Fantasy appears from the outside-in, healthy imagination emerges from inside-out. Sadly, most often what 'chooses us' is not in our best mental, emotional, and spiritual interest. Fantasy is void of real substance and is full of empty exaggerations. It is the root of self-destructive temptation and behavior when it has control over the mind.

All of the fantasy images, that we encounter and absorb, collect in the subconscious layers of our identity and shape a backdrop or lens through which we apprehend and interpret the world. This backdrop, in turn, becomes the source of our automatic and reactive behavioral patterns, stimulated by the ego's self-centered drive for survival and instant gratification. Keep in mind that this lens is being molded from the moment of birth, and even prior (from immersion in the Mikvah. See, *Ramah*, Yoreh De'ah, 198: 48. *Shach* ad loc. *Rokeach* and the *KolBo*,, Hilchos Niddah). For this reason, what one's awareness sees when it looks through this lens is a kaleidoscope of potential ways to feed and aggrandize the ego. One's environment seems full of enticements and repulsions, which the ego wants to indulge or avoid. The self becomes unsteady as it is pulled or pushed from one stimulus to another. From the soul's perspective, all of these potential ego-aggrandizements are recognized as illusory temptations and distractions from a person's ultimate purpose. The soul knows that they are unhealthy impulses, or at least spiritually unproductive ones, with their false images and fantastic impressions.

However, very often, a person may have a negative subconscious image which tells him that he is not capable of living up his higher self or greatness, even though on a conscious level he believes that he can. Your inner self-image is formed by your upbringing, education, culture, and personal experiences. It is comprised of a complex combination of nature and nurture; in fact, many people refer to it as our 'second-nature.' It is 'who' takes the wheel when we go on 'auto-pilot.' If this image is of a 'worthless' person, meaning that if you think of yourself deep-down as worthless, you will indeed often act 'worthless.' Such a negative self-image, which can stubbornly evade and resist even the most well-intentioned words and ideas, can be more effectively addressed using the tools of visualization and other methods of rectified imagination. That is simply because our subconscious speaks in the language of images, rather than ideas.

When you learn to harness your *Chush haTziyur* / sense of imagination, you can access and affect your psyche more deeply and directly than conventional study (Rabbi Simcha Zissel of Kelm, *Kisvei ha-Saba miKelm*, 1, p.143-144; Rabbi Eliyahu Dessler, *Michtav me-Eliyahu*, 1, p. 296 and 4 p. 252-253). Self-transformation is simply more effective when you can vividly visualize your goal.

When we thus gain control over our *Dimyon* / imaginative power, we can creatively curate the images and identity that are consistent with our deepest truth. Only then can we truly begin to be inwardly redeemed. Until this point we are only able to work on ourselves from the outside-in. No matter how deep an idea is, it ultimately is unable to transform our subconscious core; this requires us to renew our catalog of internal imagery. At first, we need to exchange unconsciously absorbed negative imagery with consciously selected positive images. By proactively choosing to generate positive imagery we are substituting one set of uncontrolled, un-chosen, and mostly unhealthy images, with carefully chosen, creative, holy, healthy imagery. In this way we are able to design a new 'set' or 'backdrop' for our reality-play.

This process radically transforms our spiritual makeup and self-image from the inside out. The deliberately positive, productive, holy, and empowering imagery begins to cancel out the old imagery related to oneself and the world that was unconsciously absorbed over the course of life. The toxic and debilitating effects of the negative self-images are thus counteracted and neutralized. Instead of helplessly projecting and living out the predictable patterns of a negative self-image, we can begin to live consciously and creatively from a place of health, wealth, and knowledge of self.

Relatedly, the Kuzari teaches that the definition of a *Chasid / truly pious person* is a person who has complete control over his or her Dimyon. Such a person is able to conjure up images in his imagination with ease; for example, meta-historical events like the Exodus from Egypt or the revelation of the Torah on Mt. Sinai. It is through this power of imagination that the Chasid is able to truly *experience* the ideas of Divine love and awe (*Kuzari*, 3:5). Similarly, Rabbi Yechezkel Levenstein teaches that a Tzadik is someone who has the ability to visualize holy things in his mind as vividly as if they were real (*Sichas Musar*, 26). We all have this power to some extent, and it is absolutely necessary to exercise it if we truly desire to refine ourselves and change the world for the better. Without it, we are left with only good ideas, which are but fingers pointing at the moon. Through the rectified imagination, however, we gain the internal ability to look past the external finger to perceive the moon itself, and beyond.

Elul, the sign of Virgo, provides us with just such an image of purity. This suggests that during Elul we should, as vividly as possible, each imagine ourselves as a *Tzadik*, someone consistently living from a place of true purity. In this context, we should practice imagining the full expression of our spiritual greatness and creative potential. Ultimately, we become what we imagine ourselves to be. Imagine yourself as a Tzadik, at least for short periods throughout the day, and you will eventually become one.

Re-Imagining your Greatness

We will now provide a few examples of such visualization practices as taught by our Sages throughout the ages.*

Rabbi Eliyahu ben Moshe diVidas, the great Sixteenth Century moralist and Kabbalist, writes in his work, *Reishis Chochmah,* that during the daily prayers we should imagine ourselves standing in Gan Eden with the souls of righteous people (*Sha'ar haKedusha,* Chapter 4). For example, one might imagine Davenning in the presence of Moshe Rabbeinu, Rabbi Akiva, Rashi or the Baal Shem Tov, surrounded and filled by the shimmering beauty of paradise and the uplifting energy of such spiritual masters.

Additionally, Rebbe Elimelech of Lizensk teaches a practice where one visualizes himself praying in the Beis Hamikdash (*Noam Elimelech,* Lech Lecha, p. 19). This visualization seems to have been practiced by Sages hundreds of years prior to Reb Elimelech, and there are thus sources for this practice in both Chasidic and non-Chasidic texts (*Yesod Shoresh haAvodah,* Sha'ar haKorban, p. 82. See also: The Rebbe RaYatz, *Igros Kodesh* Vol. 8, p 200, and R. Klunimus Kalmish of Peasetzna, *Hachsharas haAvreichim,* 4).

The point of this visualization is to imaginally experience yourself standing in the Temple, or even in the innermost chamber of the Holy of Holies, the most sacred of spaces. This practice is even deeper than imagining yourself being surrounded by *Tzadikim,* as in the visualization suggested above, for here, you are the *Tzadik* — the holiest person in the world.

* For a more detailed account of these and other traditional visualization practices, see the book: *Visualization and Imagery: Harnessing the Power of the Mind's Eye*

Within our deepest source, in our *Pintele / innermost point* or *Shoresh haNeshamah /* root of the soul, we are each indeed Tzadikim, as we are, on that fundamental level, always already at one with our Source, basking within the Infinite Light of Hashem. From this perspective, Rabbi Chayim Vital (*Sha'arei Kedusha,* 3:5) writes, "A person should turn his attention away from all physicality and conjure up an image of ascending into the upper worlds. He should have the intention to receive the light from the source of his soul, where his soul comes from...."

There is the 'imperfect self' and a 'perfect self.' We are a composite of both, neither completely one nor the other. There is a part of the self that is still imperfect and we are working towards perfecting it, and there is a part of the self that is always and forever perfect. We are thus both perfect and imperfect at the same time. This is an essential teaching to keep in mind during the month of Elul, while we are engaged in such deep, and sometimes difficult, work of self-reflection and spiritual transformation.

Our imperfect self is the self, as manifest in the world, a composite of our imperfect actions or inactions, our imperfect or unconscious speech, and our imperfect or negative thoughts. This lower self is constantly evolving. Hopefully, it is progressing rather than regressing, as it moves from the lower level of *Nefesh /* egoic instincts to the ascending levels of *Ruach /* spirit and *Neshamah /* soul. This is the part of the self that is constantly striving, aspiring, and developing; this is the level of self that we are working on refining during Elul.

Our 'perfect self,' the level of *Yechidah* / Unique Oneness, is always whole, pure and unified with the Ultimate Perfection of Hashem. This is our unmoving essence, represented by our 'inner Yud' (the letter of the month), as discussed previously.

Struggles, ups and downs, falls and recoveries are all part of living from the perspective of the lower, striving self. On this level, we are born into a sense of lack and always in search for greater fulfillment. But we should not forget that we can also live from the perspective of unchanging purity, wholeness, and perfection, above and beyond all struggle, striving, and ambition. Here, because we are already in perfect unity, there is no reason to struggle and there is nowhere to go. This is the level of soul that we must never lose sight or hold of, especially during the month of Elul when we are more focused on our imperfections and mistakes than most other times. By remaining connected to this 'Besula' aspect of ourselves even while we are 'in the field' and doing the hard work of Teshuvah, we are able to remain rooted in a higher, healthier, and holier perspective, allowing us to maintain our ultimate faith and hope in ourselves and, even more importantly, in Hashem.

Elul is on one hand inevitably a time for *Gevurah* / strength and discipline, where one constructively criticizes and demands more of oneself in order to grow and move forward. But we also need to make sure we balance this out with *Chesed* / loving-kindness and acceptance, wherein we also acknowledge our achievements and accomplishments. On the deepest level, there is a part of us that is always perfect and can never become sullied, and the more we live from that place, the more our imperfections are in fact perfected.

In the simplest terms, just as you used to unconsciously fantasize about sin and compulsively obsess about your shortcomings, now, with the aid of these practices, you can consciously visualize yourself performing acts of selfless goodness and fully actualized potential. In this way, you can 'reset' and 'reprogram' those previously ingrained patterns of your imagination and lay the foundation for a new, improved and refined 'second nature.'

In conclusion, the month of Elul is represented by the zodiac symbol of *Besula* / Virgo. This energy manifests in two ways. During the course of Elul, through the gradual, refining process of *Teshuvah*, we work to reclaim our innate 'virgin' purity. More importantly, however, this month serves to remind us of the indestructible purity that already exists within us. Although at times obscured or neglected, this part of us never goes away — we are always essentially whole. During the month of Elul, our work is to chip away at our *Kelipos* / hardened shells of 'character armor,' so that we can reveal this ever-present purity within.

☾

℣ PRACTICES:
Using the tools of the month to finish the year strong

PRACTICE 1:
You Are a Tzadik

ITHIN EACH ONE OF US THERE IS AN UNSULLIED CORE of perfection, a concealed Tzadik-point. To live an optimal life, we need to learn to imagine ourselves as a Tzadik and live from that place of perfect purity (*Tzav veZiruz* 24, p.340). Regarding this, the Rebbe MaHaRaSh, the fourth Chabad Rebbe, says that every person should imagine themselves as a Tzadik for at least fifteen minutes a day.

This is not simply an affirmation, nor mere fantasy, it is true. You are a tzadik. Maybe it is not true in the way you have lived at all moments and under all conditions, but in essence it is true. This because there is a small sliver of Infinity, of Hashem's Presence, within each one of us — a point of ultimate perfection and infinite unity.

You can view yourself as a *Rasha* / damaged soul and struggle with that self-image. Or you can realize that there is a Tzadik within you — a still, small portion of perfection and goodness — and aspire to live up to that image. Instead of subscribing to your negative, false fantasy of being a Rasha, use your *Dimyon* / power of imagination to tap into who you truly are, a Tzadik.

Clearly it is more productive and healthy on all levels to see yourself according to the perspective of your true potential, and aspire to live up to that image. Seeing yourself as a weak person, and then struggling against yourself, only weakens you further. Arguing for and defending your smallness and limitations will ensure that you remain limited and small. The world and others around us are also best served when we envision ourselves at our best, and thus manifest our Tzadik qualities.

This mindset is worthwhile as a general outlook on life: you are a Tzadik,, already able to transcend your issues and struggles with ease; just act from that place. This mindset is also effective in relation to very specific issues. Say, for instance, a person is working on overcoming his instinct to flare up in anger. He should imagine himself as if he has already perfected that very attribute and pattern, and approach subsequent experiences of anger from that paradigm (*Michtav M'eliyahu* 5, p. 38).

Take a few minutes right now to visualize yourself as a Tzadik. From this perspective, recall a couple of the traits that you are working on. See yourself with those traits already deeply refined. What do you see? How do you feel?

Now visualize yourself as a perfect Tzadik in all aspects. Remember, this is already true from a soul perspective. What do you see? How do you feel? Then, from this place, conclude your practice and immediately go do a good deed — something small, but one that would befit a Tzadik. Then, repeat this action.

Kavanah

Invite all of yourself.

In a comfortable seat, take a moment to let go of all the noise, chaos and movement in your life; simply be. Gently move your awareness into your inner world.

You may notice sounds, sensations, thoughts or feelings coming and going. Sense everything without manipulating it; simply accept what is, and relax the urge to act.

Bring to mind any self-identifying labels or definitions, i.e., I am the son or daughter of so and so. I do this or that professionally. I am short, tall, thin, heavy. I am learned, skilled, talented. Without thinking about them in detail, bring to mind all the things that you have and all the things that you do.

Now, dig a little deeper, ask yourself, "Who am I? If I am not my possessions, my feelings, or even my thoughts, so then, who am I?"

A label or a self-definition is only a thought, and you are not your thoughts.

So then, ask yourself again, "Who am I?"

With each inhale go deeper, and with every exhale shed the layers of your constructed personality.

With each new exhalation, release every single label with which you identify in all of its familiarity, safety, comfort and power of habit.

As the external identities are shed, make an affirmation of this specific insight: I am not my body, I am not what I do, I am not what I have,

I am not my thoughts, I am not my feelings,

I am not my labels, I am not my limitations,
I am at the threshold of my deepest core.

This inner core, this Neshamah, is my true identity.

This is my point of origin. This is who and what and why I am.

Always remember: You are a soul within a body, not a body that has a soul. This infinite soul resides in the deep place within that is always pure and whole. Your authentic self is Ohr/light, meaning, connection, unity, and perfection. This is you! As the inhalations continue, go deeper and deeper. Allow your exhalations to radiate this light outwards and embrace the world.

As you exhale, ground your feet, rooting down physically and spiritually as you illuminate your surroundings from within. Grounding yourself on your exhalations provides more freedom of movement and flexibility to your upper body, especially around your heart. Allow each exhale to shine outward, in front of you and behind.

Now, immediately proceed to do a positive deed, a Mitzvah. It could be something small, but something befitting for a Tzadik to do. Repeat this action, or another appropriate one, a few times over the next few hours.

☾

PRACTICE 2:
Reviewing and Refining the Entire Past Year

A FULL CUP CANNOT BE FILLED. TO PROPERLY PREPARE ourselves to enter into Rosh Hashanah and the New Year, we need to mindfully put the old year to rest. One important method for this is called *Cheshbon haNefesh* / accounting of the soul. In this process we survey the past year and each major experience, and take responsibility for it. After we have gathered up and held our past in all its details, we can let it all go, empty the cup, and move forward to receive the fullness and promise of the future.

We have learned that Elul is a time to focus on forgiveness — forgiveness for ourselves, for our family, for our community, for our people, and for the world. We seek forgiveness for our own misdeeds and miscommunications, as well as to forgive those who have, consciously or unconsciously, trespassed against us. It is therefore very helpful to keep a journal during this period, noting major breakthroughs and events from the past year, along with our reactions to them, and envisioning how we would respond in the future when living as the 'Tzadik' that we essentially are.

In general, this practice of Cheshbon haNefesh includes asking yourself tough questions. For example, 'What have I been doing with my life?' 'Where is my life heading?' 'Am I living my purpose?' 'Am I living my fullest potential?' 'Have I been honest with myself and others?' 'Have I grown during the past year?' 'Where can I still improve?'

A thorough, in-depth Cheshbon haNefesh requires us to go through and examine the past year month by month. If you write consistently in a personal journal throughout the year, you can simply go through the year week by week and day by day to review and revisit your thoughts, words, and actions of note and consequence. In this chapter, we will provide a guided Cheshbon according to the quality of each particular month. We will also organize and contextualize the details of this spiritual accounting in a way that you can perform it even if you do not have total command of your memories from the past year.

As we are exploring throughout the *Spiral of Time* series of books, each month of the year has a unique archetypal quality. For example, Iyyar is a month connected to healing and Teves to relationships. And so, when reviewing the month of Teves from the past year you can think about your interpersonal relationships during this month; or alternatively, when you focus on Teves in the course of this practice, you can think about all your relationships from the entire year. Additionally, you can think about all your issues with healing in the month of Iyyar specifically, or you can broaden the concept to include all your health issues from throughout the entire year, as you focus on the month of Iyyar. The awareness of each month's quality therefore serves to focus your attention on that month, as well as to provide an archetypal perspective on the entire year.

The inner work of Cheshbon haNefesh is certainly appropriate for any day of Elul. However, it is especially important for the final 12 days of the month, as each of these days correspond to one of the 12 months of the year (Rebbe Rayatz, *Sefer HaSichos*, 5703, p. 177). With this in mind, one can focus their Cheshbon haNefesh on a single month and its resident archetypal quality for each of the concluding 12 days of the month leading up to Rosh Hashanah.

It is important to note that Elul comes at the end of the solar cycle. Nisan is the first month of the lunar year, as counted by the Hebrew calendar. The first 12 days of Nisan therefore correspond to the 12 months of the upcoming year (*Igra d'K ala*, Pikudei), in the same way that the last 12 days of Elul correspond to the year that has passed. During that time we should envision and project positivity and blessing for the upcoming year. We can see from these two periods of 12 days that any time of physical or spiritual transition can be an opportunity to take account of our lives and to resolve the past or bring light into the future.

The following Cheshbon practice will be structured according to the order of the months, focusing our awareness of their corresponding energetic qualities, and providing us with relevant suggested questions and prompts for deeper self-evaluation and reflection.

☾

KAVANAH / Mindful Intention 2:
A Review of the Past Year:

Set a soft timer, in order to fully enter this practice without thinking about time. You can be fully present. Allow yourself the gift of this experience.

If you are new to this type of practice, you might start with 10-20 minutes. However, this is not a 'competitive' practice, so if that amount of time feels overwhelming, it is best to start smaller, and steadily build on a strong foundation.

In a comfortable seat, preferably with your eyes closed, take a moment to let go of all the noise, chaos, and movement in your life; simply be and breathe. Gently move into your inner world.

You may notice sounds, sensations, thoughts, or feelings coming and going. Sense everything without manipulating it; simply accept what is, and relax the urge to act.

Watch and feel yourself slowly breathing in and out. Bring awareness to your body.

Then begin moving your awareness further inward.

Now begin to review your past year, month by month and archetype by archetype, starting with last year's Tishrei, the first month of the year:

TISHREI (September-October):
Resolutions and Commitments

During this time, summer is ending, and a New Year is beginning.

Think about the resolutions or intentions you took upon yourself last year during Tishrei, the High Holiday season.

What commitments did you make or contemplate? What goals did you set?

Have you achieved them?

Now think about all the resolutions you took upon yourself throughout the course of the entire year. Did you resolve at any point to exercise more regularly?

To study more Torah? To be more patient?

Did you accomplish any of these goals, or were you lax in following through?

How did you do? Be honest, but not harsh.

Next, move on to the month of Cheshvan.

CHESHVAN (October-November):
Transitions

During this period the seasons change, fall begins turning into winter.

It gets colder and darker.

Cheshvan is all about transitions, moving from one phase to the next.

Think about the transitions in your life that occurred last year in Cheshvan.

Now expand this focus to the entire year.

Think about all the transitions you experienced over the course of the past year. Maybe it was the loss of a loved one or the birth of a child, a lost or new job.

Which transitions were of your own doing and which were circumstantial?

How did you respond to the challenges of these changes?

What were your conscious choices and what were your more subconscious reactions?

Be honest and aware of the big picture.

Next, move on to the month of Kislev.

KISLEV (November-December): *Miracles*

The winter solstice occurs towards the end of Kislev, when the first glimmer of growing sunlight appears in the Northern Hemisphere. This returning of the light represents the world of miracles, the extraordinary and the unexpected.

First consider: Are you open to the possibility of Divine miracles, or do you find yourself attributing everything in your life to natural causes and conditions?

Is nature itself not miraculous?

Then, think about any 'miracles' that occurred to you in Kislev.

Acknowledge and express your gratitude for each one.

Now, expand this theme to the entire year.

Think about all the 'miracles' in your life.

What extraordinary or unexpected events happened to you over the course of the past year?

Did you find a spouse, fall in love, land a dream job, or make a significant breakthrough?

How did you respond to these Divine gifts? Did you integrate them into your life? Were you grateful and did you express thanks for them as they occurred?

Did you pray for the fulfilment of your needs and wants, and those of others?

Be honest and humble.

Next, move on to the month of Teves.

TEVES (December-January): *Relationships*

Teves is the coldest month of the year, impelling us to seek human warmth and contact; the focus of this month is thus interpersonal relationships.

Think about how you related to others in Teves.

Call to mind (and heart) your various relationships with parents, siblings, spouse, children, friends, co-workers, even 'enemies.'

Acknowledge and express gratitude for each one.

Now expand this idea to the entire year.

Did you improve your relationships? If so, which ones?

Did you focus on what you could give, or only on what you could get?

Where did you fall short in your relationships? Where were your areas of success?

Be honest and forgiving.

Next, move on to the month of Shevat.

SHEVAT (January-February): *Eating*

In Shevat the cold of winter abates slightly, and this stimulates the appetite.

Thus Shevat is connected to eating and consuming.

Eating is one of the primary appetites that we must work on to refine our character and live a truly conscious spiritual life.

Think for a moment about your relationship to food during the month of Shevat.

Did you notice any shift of appetite or awareness during this time?

Now extend this focus to the entire year.

How was your relationship to food this past year?

Healthy? Obsessive? Disciplined? Neurotic?

Were you able to let go and enjoy yourself when appropriate?

Were you able to exert your will and define your boundaries when necessary?

Do a serious and thorough evaluation of your relationship to food over the past year.

Be honest and nurturing.

Now, move on to the month of Adar.

ADAR (February-March): Joy

Adar, coming at the end of the cold winter, is a month of joy and holy laughter.

Recall whether or not you were happy in Adar.

If so, was there any particular reason you can identify for you happiness?

If not, did you attempt to shift your mood, or just accept your depressed state?

Now extend this focus to the entire year.

What were the truly joyous moments of your past year?

What made you laugh? What made you sing? What made you dance?

Did you grow or learn from the joy you experienced in the past year?

Was your joy dependent upon external stimuli, conditions or persons, or did you cultivate it from within?

How did you react when you didn't feel joyous?

How did you contribute to the happiness of others?

Be honest and happy.

Now, move on to the month of Nisan.

NISAN (March-April):
Redemption and Liberation

Nisan is the beginning of spring, a time of energetic revival and physical renewal following the cold of winter.

Appropriately, the spiritual energies of this month also guide us to greater freedom and new life.

Think about your experience of Nisan.

Were you redeemed or renewed on some level?

How did the onset of spring affect you?

Now broaden this focus to include the entire year.

Think about the issues or constrictions that you needed to release this past year: certain difficulties that you overcame, particular patterns or habits that you broke, relationships you evolved out of — or evolved within.

Did you attain a more enhanced feeling of freedom this past year?

If not, what else might you still need to do to achieve a deeper level of personal redemption?

Be honest and courageous.

Now, move on to the month of Iyyar.

IYYAR (April-May): *Healing*

Iyyar brings pleasant weather and is connected to all forms of healing:

physical, mental, emotional, spiritual, and relational.

Think about the healing that you allowed to occur in the month of Iyyar.

Were there any particular dimensions of your life that achieved greater integration during this month?

Now think about your health and well-being throughout the past year.

The deepest healing is being true to yourself on every level.

What ailments or challenges did you experience over the past year?

What did you do to help or hinder your own healing process?

Be honest and healthy.

Now, move on to the month of Sivan.

SIVAN (May-June): *Torah*

The month of Sivan is dedicated to the revelation of Torah.

Begin by thinking about your Sivan this past year; were you open to 'receive the Torah'?

What did you learn throughout the year?

How was the quality and quantity of your spiritual studies?

What wisdom did you gain?

How have you integrated the teachings you have learned?

Be honest and open to receive.

Next, move on to the month of Tamuz.

TAMUZ (June-July): *Destruction*

Tamuz is a month connected to all forms of destruction and endings.

It was during this month that the walls of the Temple were breached.

Although the Temple does not completely fall until the month of Av, we meditate on the beginnings of its disintegration during the month of Tamuz.

Think about all the things that fell apart during your past year.

What have you lost? Whom have you lost? How are you dealing with these losses?

Although this may be a painful area to explore, it is integral to our rebuilding.

Be honest and gentle.

Next, move on to the month of Av.

AV (July-August): *Reconciliation*

The deeper level of Av, and especially the second half of the month, is related to building and reconciling after destruction has occurred.

Although most commonly characterized by the total destruction of both the First and Second Temples during the first half of the month, we also need to focus on the question, "What next?"

This is because 'Moshiach is born on Tisha b'Av.'

The day of deepest destruction is thus also the beginning of redemption and rebuilding.

Begin by thinking about the month of Av in particular; did anything come to an end and/or begin to reconfigure during this time?

Now expand this focus to the entire year. What restorative steps did you pursue with regard to broken areas in your life?

How did you try to repair or redeem broken aspects of yourself, your relationships, and the world over the past year?

Did you volunteer any of your time or energy to people in need?

Have you taken time to reach out to someone you have not been in contact with for a long time?

Be honest and hopeful.

Now, move on to the final month of the year, the present month, Elul.

ELUL (August-September): *Soul Searching*

As we are performing a *Cheshbon haNefesh* / spiritual accounting of the past year, it is a good time to also think about the concept of Cheshbon haNefesh itself.

Have you been honest with yourself this past year?

Were you able to look at your life deeply, critically, and frequently?

Were you able to judge yourself favorably and lovingly?

Think about the times that you were really honest with yourself. How did it feel?

Think about the times when you were dishonest with yourself or others.

How did that feel?

Be honest and accepting.

ೞ
ENDING STRONG:

ONCE YOU HAVE GONE THROUGH THE ENTIRE YEAR, OWNING up to and taking full responsibility for all of your mishaps and successes, now it is time to move into a more proactive consciousness. Look at this present moment as the gift of a new beginning. Resolve to make amends and deal better with these twelve archetypal points during the coming year. Write down your resolutions and keep them in a place where you will see them on a regular basis.

Begin with the month of Tishrei, and the importance of *resolutions and commitments*. Resolve that this coming year you are going to be more mindful and in touch with your resolutions and commitments. You are going to be more focused and creative in keeping them. You are going to follow through with greater strength and conviction of character.

Next move onto the month of Cheshvan, and this month's theme of *transitions*. Resolve to be more mindful and present with all the various transitions that will come up during the coming year, such as a new job, home, or relationship. Flexibility and maintaining a process-orientation are both key to navigating periods of transition. Commit yourself to flow with an open mind and heart.

Next move on to the month of Kislev, and the idea of *miracles*. Resolve to be more grateful for all the events in your life. Resolve to see the miracles around you every moment. Resolve to demonstrate your gratitude to the Master of the universe for any unexpected changes for the better that will come to you, G-d willing.

Now move on to the quality of the month of Teves, the area of *relationships*. Resolve to work on your interpersonal relationships and friendships, and to be a more supportive and present friend, spouse, child, parent, student / teacher in this coming year.

At this point turn to the month of Shevat, and your approach to *eating and food*. Resolve to have a healthier relationship with eating and food; to eat healthier, more mindfully and for a higher purpose. Make plans on how you will be more disciplined and less obsessive about food or other objects that you consume or internalize.

Now think about *joy*, the quality of the month of Adar. Resolve to connect frequently and strongly with whatever brings you true happiness. What decisions do you need to make in order to create steady, balanced joy for yourself and others in your life?

The month of Nisan is connected with *redemption and liberation*. Resolve to utilize and integrate the tools and practices that bring you inner freedom. Don't be satisfied with mere temporary experiences of freedom. How, exactly, will you commit to your best path of lasting, pervasive liberation from negativity, limitation, and untruth?

Now move on to the month of Iyyar, and the aspect of *healing*. Resolve to work on healing yourself on all levels during this coming year: physical, mental, emotional, spiritual, interpersonal, and global. Set specific goals and actions that will move you toward those goals.

Sivan is connected to *Torah, Divine Wisdom*, and learning. Resolve to make more time for learning this year. Commit yourself to better integrating all the teachings and wisdom you receive from this learning, and from others you encounter. Open your mind and heart to see and hear Torah in unlikely places. Resolve to research and delve into the area of Torah study that is most enlivening for you.

Next, move on to the month of Tamuz and the theme of *destruction*. Resolve to be more mindful and compassionate in any experience of destruction that you may encounter this coming year. Resolve that you will process any losses with directness, resiliency, empathy, and wisdom.

Av is a month of *reconciliation*. Resolve to work during this coming year on reconciling with others and repairing your world. If you have been out of touch or in conflict with someone, reach out to them. Resolve to volunteer your time and energy to people in need, especially those people who most need to be 'reconciled' with your community or society.

Now move into the final month of the year, the present month of Elul, and the process of *soul searching*. Resolve to be more self-reflective and honest throughout this coming year. Commit to smaller practices of *Cheshbon haNefesh* on a daily, weekly or monthly basis. Resolve also to judge yourself more favorably and lovingly, and to grow into and align with the 'Tzadik' that you already are.

As the new year is about to ensue, with its entirely new Divine revelation, we need to seriously take the idea of renewal to heart. To this effect, it would do us well to meditate on the words of the great 13th Century rabbi and moralist, Rabbeinu Yonah: *"The foundation of Teshuvah is considering today as the very day you were born, the first day of your life, and you have no demerits or merits."* This state of consciousness is both the foundation and the goal of Teshuvah.

Rosh Hashanah will be the simultaneous downloading of all the potential days, hours and minutes of the following year. Flowing out from Rosh Hashanah, every moment of the year is completely new. The *Ko'ach Hischadshus* / power of renewal is present within every moment of creation. There are no two moments alike. We need to "consider today as the very day we were born," because today, and this very moment, is in fact entirely new.

The sense of being aware of the miraculous novelty of this very moment is essential, specifically when it comes to the end of the year. As we learned in the beginning of this volume, Elul is the *Acharis* / end or back of the year. We all love to start projects and we often do so with enthusiasm, but, as a project drags on we begin to lose focus; there is a dulling of excitement and we become too tired or distracted to finish. The sensation of the project being in the Acharis stage, that you have had enough and you just want to move on to the next project, sets in right when you are close to the finish line. That is why many people can start projects, but far fewer can see them through.

At the end of the year, many people also struggle with a linguistically related quality, *Aichur* / lateness. They put off their Cheshbon haNefesh until the very last moment. Both of these tendencies (ending and lateness) relate to the left hand, the body part of the month. The left side is symbolic of habitual or subconscious patterns, drives and passions. And this is precisely why, at the end of the year, we need to become more aware of the constant renewal and the *Chidush* / novelty of every moment. Nothing is ever actually old. Only our 'habitual mind' makes it seem so. Everything is entirely fresh, and has never been as it is at this very moment.

Ending also gives rise to nostalgia, and with that, sadness. As we are about to end something in our lives, even if it is a healthy ending, we sometimes become a little sad. When a job ends, or a relationship, or G-d forbid, a marriage, people start mulling over the past, thinking, 'If I had only done such and such differently.' Such regrets and questions of 'what if' can bring about melancholy, laziness and a depletion of energy.

In Elul, we need to contend with both the senses of oldness and melancholy as well as their accompanying spiritual depletion. Thus, according to the Shulchan Aruch and Sefardic practice, one must awake especially early throughout Elul to recite *Selichos* / prayers for forgiveness. Waking up early counters the natural laziness and *Aichur* that can set in at this time of year.

This is also the reason we blow the Shofar every day of Elul (except the last day). The sounds of the Shofar awaken us and give us new *Chayus* / life and vitality. Besides the effect of hearing the sound, the act of taking an inanimate, lifeless horn and blowing our breath into it and creating sound is a symbolic act of revival. Inwardly, we become more alive and awakened by the act of enlivening and animating something (or someone) outside of ourselves. All this gives us more strength to end the year with vitality, enthusiasm, and hope.

The *Avodah* / work of Elul is to wake up from our spiritual slumber and perceive life with freshness and a sense of the newness of every moment. The letter of the month is Yud and in terms of grammar, the prefix of a Yud makes a verb into a continuous action occurring both in the present as well as on into the future (*Iyov*, 1:5. See *Rashi*, *Shemos*, 15:1). It takes a word that could mean a past action, such as עשה /*Asah* / done, and turns it into יעשה /*Ya'ase* / doing or will do. Yud thus represents the renewal of any concept. As the year is ending, we need to focus on the miraculous newness of the present moment, so we will have the strength to wrap up the nearly complete year, without jumping blindly into the future. When we end the past year with strength, consciousness, awareness and patience, we can begin the new year with greater clarity, conviction, and creativity.

☾

ༀ
SUMMARY OF ELUL

*I*N THE MONTH OF ELUL, SUMMER VACATIONS ARE ENDING and people start focussing on the new year to come. The Tikkun of this autumnal **season** thus includes reviewing the past year, making amends and doing Teshuvah so we can move forward from a good place. The **Torah portions** of this period and the **verse** of the month both teach us about this inner work of Teshuvah and support us in our transformative pursuits during this time. Action, appropriately, is the '**sense**' of the month; as our consciousness is actively focused on reviewing our past deeds and refining ourselves in preparation for the coming year. Our actions during Elul must therefore be geared towards rectifying our subconscious mind, symbolized by the left hand, the **body part** of the month.

This requires a self-generated 'awakening from below,' represented and evoked by the month's permutational **sequence of Hashem's name.** There is no external stimulus of a holiday in Elul, and in that sense the spiritual atmosphere is cold and dry like the **element** of earth. However, the **name of the month** itself reveals that we are empowered to "carefully search" ourselves with the energetic quality of a "shout of joy." When we do so, we can tap into our innermost point of essential purity, symbolized by the **zodiac** sign of *Besulah* / Virgo (the Virgin), and the **letter** Yud. Then, from this indestructible essence within, we can let go of the past year and embrace the future with renewed faith and hope.

12 DIMENSIONS OF ELUL	
Sequence of Hashem's Name	*Hei-Hei-Vav-Yud*
Verse	"*U-tzedakaH tihiyeH lanU kiY...* / And it will be a merit to us if…" (*Devarim* 6:25)
Letter	Yud
Month Name	'Shout for Joy' or 'Carefully Search'
Sense	*Asiyah* / action
Zodiac	*Besulah* / Virgo
Tribe	Gad
Body Part	Left hand (subconscious mind)
Element	Earth
Parshios /Torah Portions	Shoftim-Nitzavim (themes of Teshuvah)
Season	End of Summer
Holiday	None

APPENDIX:
Two Essays on Elul

APPENDIX 1:

I-IT, I-YOU, I-I
Three Modes of Human & Divine Encounter

ELUL IS AN OPPORTUNE TIME TO WORK ON OUR RELATION-
SHIP with HaKadosh Baruch Hu. When we do so with
diligence and discipline, we can give birth to a deeper and
higher level of relationship with ourselves, with others, and with
Hashem in the coming year.

Let us briefly review what we have learned above in the section
on the Holidays of the Month, as it describes our developing relationship with Hashem. Rosh Hashanah represents the sixth day of
creation, the day Hashem created humanity, and therefore the first
day of creation is the 25th of Elul. These dates represent stages in
the prenatal formation of a child in the womb. The actual birth of
the child will occur in Nisan, the first month of the year.

The creation of the human being on Rosh Hashanah represents
the first moment that the 'fetus' attains a discernible human form.

The 25th of Elul is thus a pregnant moment just prior to the development of most of the defining human traits; it is also when the heartbeat first appears. Medically, the heartbeat is said to be discernible roughly 40 days after conception. Forty days prior to the 25th of Elul is the 15th of Av. This day, Tu b'Av, is therefore the climactic moment of intimate embrace, creative conception, and the first glimmer of love that the parents feel for the future child.

Tu b'Av is thus the first 'revelation' within Hashem of a Divine desire to create a 'child,' a world, humanity — to initiate a relationship with a veritable other. The month of Elul is thus the time in which we are growing and developing 'in-utero.' This is precisely why we need to go deep and work on ourselves in this month, in preparation for our birth into a new, closer relationship with our Creator.

Three Levels of Nearness

There are three modes of relationship, both with others and with HaKadosh Baruch Hu. We will call them: 'I-it,' 'I-you,' and 'I-I.' An 'I-it' relationship is when we encounter another as an 'it,' an object — something or someone to use. An encounter with the seat we are sitting on is an 'I-it' relationship. It is useful to us. Sadly, many encounters between people are strictly 'I-it' relationships. This is what is commonly referred to as 'objectifying' another person, to relate to them only as an object of utility, devoid of their own substance and significance. Even when we benefit another person, we might still see them as an 'it,' an impersonal receiver or even a statistic or means of meeting our quota, *Chas veShalom* / Heaven forbid. We must therefore constantly guard against this tendency to view others as mere means to our desired ends.

A deeper level of relationship is 'I-you.' This is a real person-to-person encounter. On this level, you are sensitive to the subjectivity of the other. He or she is a real person to you, complete with their own story and soul reality. You therefore take their needs personally, you listen attentively to their words and even what is behind their words. In this level, there is a real connection and real love.

Even still, the deepest level of relationship is 'I-I.' On this level, your 'I' becomes one with the other's 'I.' Not only are you aware that the other is not an 'it,' but that they are not essentially a separate 'you' either, you are on some level interconnected and even interdependent. An 'I-I' encounter is the realization that the two seemingly separate entities interacting are really one.

Our relationship with Hashem can also be on the level of 'I-it.' In this perspective, Hashem is a totally separate, impersonal Creator, King, or Judge. On this level, Hashem is utterly beyond me and I am only able to stand in awe of the Infinite Majesty and magnitude of the Creator and His Creation. This is the mode of *Yiras Hashem* / awe of the Transcendent One. I am a servant and Hashem is my Master.

An 'I-you' relationship with Hashem is deeply personal. Hashem is experienced as immanent, close, and lovingly responsive — the Living G-d. On this level, I feel very close to HaKadosh Baruch Hu, sometimes as a child encountering my affectionate Parent, sometimes even as my intimate Lover. This is the experience of *Ahavas Hashem* / love of the Beloved.

Beyond even that exalted level is the 'I-I' relationship with Hashem. This is an encounter with the radically nondual nature of Hashem, in which there is no separation between the small 'i' and the Great 'I,' the Only 'I'. On this level, Hashem is both transcendent and immanent, both 'beyond' and 'immediate,' simultaneously. On this level, awe and love are not opposite from each other, they are rather, unified as one all-inclusive experience. Realizing this mindful state of 'inclusive transcendence' gives rise to *Deveikus* / active unity.

I-It	*Yiras Hashem*	Transcendent Separation
I-You	*Ahavas Hashem*	Immanent Relation
I-I	*Deveikus*	Active Unity

Three Forms of Development in Elul

As we discussed briefly in the section focused on the name of the month, there are many acronyms formed out of the four letters of the name 'Elul' — Aleph, Lamed, Vav and Lamed. Each four-word verse alludes to a dimension of our spiritual work that we can focus on and increase during Elul: *Tefilah* / prayer, *Teshuvah* / transformation, *Tzedakah* / charity, *Torah* / Divine Wisdom, *Mesiras Nefesh* / self sacrifice, and *Simcha* / joy.

To review:

1: Prayer – *Tefilah*

"אני לדודי ודודי לי /*Ani L'dodi V'dodi Li* / I am to my Beloved and my Beloved is to me" (*Shir Hashirim*, 6:3). This verse alludes to *Tefilah* / prayer, the reaching up from below to Above.

2: Transformation – *Teshuvah*

"Then Hashem your God will open up (literally, 'circumcise') את־
לבבך ואת־לבב /*Es L'vavcha, Ves L'vav...* / your heart and the hearts
[of your offspring]" (*Devarim*, 30:6). This alludes to Teshuvah and
spiritual transformation, the opening of our hearts.

3: Charity – *Tzedakah*

"The sending of portions (of food) איש לרעהו ומתנות לאביונים /*Ish
L're'eihu, U-matanas L'evyonim* / to one's friends, and gifts to the
needy" (*Esther* 9:22). This alludes to *Tzedakah* / charity and helping
others in need.

4: Divine Wisdom – *Torah*

"אנה לידו ושמתי לך /*Eina L'yadi V'samti Lach* / And for one who
did not lie in wait [to kill premeditatedly], but Hashem has caused
it to happen, I shall establish for you a place [to which he can flee]"
(*Shemos*, 21:13). This verse refers to the Mitzvah of building cities of
refuge, which alludes to Torah-study — a refuge for the soul.

5: Sacrifice – *Mesiras Nefesh*

"אחד לעלה ואחד לחטאת /*Echad Leolah, Vechad Lachatas* / One will
be for the burnt offering and the other for the purification offering" (*Vayikra*, 12:8). This verse refers to sacrifices brought to the Holy
Temple, which allude inwardly to the concept of *Mesiras Nefesh* /
self-sacrifice, dedicating and offering our inner 'animal' on the altar.

6: Joy – *Simcha*

"Then Moshe and the Israelites sang את /*Es* this song ויאמרו לה'

לאמר / *LaHashem, Vayomru Leimor* / to Hashem, and they said" (*Shemos*, 15:1). This acronym skips two words. The Arizal, however, teaches that the four letters of Elul in this verse are actually in reverse order, in the words ויאמרו לאמר אשירה לה' /*LaHashem, Vayomru, Leimor, Ashira*. In any case, this verse alludes to the *Simcha* / joy of liberation and redemption. Each dimension of our spiritual work during Elul must be infused with joy.

We will now focus more deeply on the three acronyms alluding to *Tzedakah*, *Tefilah* and *Torah*. They each represent a primary interface through which the three dimensions of relationship with HaKadosh Baruch Hu can be developed. They can also be described as three primary movements:

Tzedakah is a movement *outward*, towards a recipient.

Tefilah is a movement *upward*, as you direct your awareness and aspirations towards Hashem and the heavens.

Torah is movement *downward and inward*, through which you draw Divine wisdom into your mind and heart.

Our relationship with Hashem in the form of *Tzedakah* is, in general, 'I-it.' That is, we are the 'it' humbly receiving Tzedakah — all our needs — from Hashem, the transcendent 'I.' Additionally, when we give Tzedakah to others, we are sometimes relating to Hashem as a Divine 'It,' a kind of cosmic vending machine that will predictably provide for us as we provide for others (*Ta'anis*, 9a).

Our relationship with Hashem in the form of *Tefilah* is, in general, 'I-You.' In Tefilah, we are given the opportunity to speak our minds and hearts to Hashem. In this way, we awaken to our own personhood, how we are feeling, and how our life is working out or not. We become a 'you' in front of the *Shomei'a Tefilos* / Listener to prayers, and draw ourselves closer to Hashem in love.

Our relationship with HaKadosh Baruch Hu in the form of Torah-study is, in general, 'I-I.' When we draw Torah down into us, and unify with the Divine wisdom within it, we become conduits of Hashem's revelation in this world. We thus become one with the Revealer. This is because essentially, "Torah, Hashem, and Israel are One" (*Zohar* 3, 73b). We are an individual 'I' encountering the Ultimate 'I.' The essence of self is unified with the Essential Self.

Besides these three general categories, there are also three sub-levels within each of the modalities of *Tzedakah, Tefilah,* and *Torah.* Each of the three interfaces similarly has its own aspect of I-it, I-you and I-I.

Three Levels within Tzedakah */ Charity*

Although Tzedakah is, in general, an I-it paradigm, there are also three levels within Tzedakah: I-it, I-you and I-I.

The I-it mode of Tzedakah: According to the Rambam, there are eight levels of Tzedakah (*Matnas Aniyim*, 10; 7-14), and the higher levels of course require the goodness of the giver's heart and a deep empathetic connection with the receiver. However, in a technical sense, the essence of Tzedakah is simply to give. From this perspective, it is not absolutely vital to consider how and why you are giving; if you give with an ulterior motive, such as in order to receive a blessing, it is still considered Tzedakah. Even if you give "so that your child should live, you are a *Tzadik Gamur* / a completely righteous person" (*Pesachim*, 8a-8b). In fact, even if money fell out of your pocket, and you did not know about it, it can still be considered Tzedakah. This is therefore a Mitzvah that can occur without intention; if you lost some money and a poor person found it, you have performed a Mitzvah. The main objective has been achieved: the poor person has been fed (*Toras Kohanim* Rashi Vayikra 5:17. Sifiri see *Rashi* to Parshas Ki Tetze 24:19). In this sense, the recipient of Tzedakah need not be encountered as a person, rather they are like an impersonal 'it.'

Here is a classic example:

Once, a wealthy disciple came to the Alter Rebbe, R. Schneur Zalman of Liadi, and said that he had been contemplating opening an orphanage, but had since abandoned the idea. Having mulled over the project he came to the realization that he was only doing it to gain more respect in his community. The Rebbe lifted his eyes and told him firmly to go ahead with the orphanage. The Rebbe said, "While perhaps you may not mean this sincerely, the poor young orphans who will eat hot meals and sleep in comfortable beds will certainly do so sincerely."

From a deeper perspective, the entire act of creation is an impersonal act of Tzedakah on the part of the Creator. Hashem had a desire to give to another entity, and therefore Hashem contracted His Infinite Essence to allow for a finite recipient to emerge. In a certain sense, Hashem was merely seeking to create an other in general, not necessarily us, meaning you or I. In this relationship,

Hashem is our Creator, who has charitably given us existence to satisfy His Own desire. Additionally, Hashem is also our 'Commander' and we are his soldiers — we are therefore somewhat impersonal recipients of His Mitzvos and commandments. *However, it is important to note that this is only one level, the lowest level, of understanding the Nature of creation.

The I-you mode of Tzedakah: In 'I-You' Tzedakah, you feel the other person's pain, and you give in response to that empathy. The Gemara says, "Tzedakah is complete only commensurate with its kindness" (*Sukah,* 49b). While simply giving qualifies as Tzedakah, what makes Tzedakah "complete" and real is *how* the giving is performed. Complete Tzedakah requires Chesed (*Rashi,* ad loc).

The I-I mode of Tzedakah: Let us understand the I-I dimension of Tzedakah with a story:

Late one cold winter night, as his family slept, Rebbe Mordechai of Nadvorna was roused from his studies when he heard a knock on the door. Opening the door, he found a lone traveler. The Rebbe immediately welcomed him inside, brought him food, started a fire, and made sure he was warm and comfortable. Even though he was unaware that he was in the home of a great Tzadik, the traveller showed discomfort when his host began to make a bed for him. "Please, don't bother," he exclaimed, "I can make the bed myself." The Rebbe responded, "My friend, I am not making the bed for you, I am making it for myself.*"*

Three Levels within Tefilah / *Prayer:*

Although Tefilah is in general an I-You paradigm, there are also three levels within Tefilah: I-It, I-you and I-I.

I-it: In prayer, we begin our relationship with Hashem in a mode of awe. HaKadosh Baruch Hu is the transcendent Reality, utterly beyond our comprehension, and we meekly bow down in surrender to Him. As we contemplate the sheer vastness of the Infinite, we begin to appreciate how distant, miniscule, and insignificant we are, like a mote of dust. Accordingly, a sense of dread can overcome us, along with an overwhelming sense of numinous presence; we suddenly realize that Hashem really does exist, it is not just a cultural belief or useful story to motivate human behavior. At that moment, we also viscerally sense the chasm between creation and its transcendent Creator. We see ourselves in comparison to an Absolute Perfection, and as a result we awaken to our alienation and distance from the Truth. This stimulates us to muster any strength we may have, and call out, "Hashem, please help us!"

I-you: Once the I-it paradigm has allowed us to perceive the existence and transcendence of the Creator, we can then move to a deeper level of prayer, in which Tefilah is an act of relating to the Divine. The root of the word *Tefilah* is *Tafel* / to adjoin, to connect in an 'I-you' mode. In prayer, we speak to Hashem in terms of Divine attributes. We do not generally pray to Hashem as a Non-Dual Reality or Formless Infinite, but rather as an 'Imminent G-d,' a 'Merciful Father,' or the 'Shield of Avraham,' who is aware of our personal predicaments and processes, who feels our pain and who listens to our prayers.

In human interactions, if you need something from someone, you might first sing their praises and then ask for the favor. If you are in touch with Hashem as infinitely vast and distant, it may seem silly to apply such a human dynamic. It may seem to inappropriately give 'form' to the Formless Absolute, and presumptuously 'make G-d in our own image.' Nevertheless, this is the internal structure of the *Nusach* / liturgy of Tefilah. So, how does this make sense? The answer is that the I-you paradigm brings us into the depths of an intimate relationship with the Divine. A 'personal' relationship happens to make Hashem even more real to us. From this perspective, Hashem is no longer the impersonal, cosmic G-d of the philosophers, but is our Loving Parent, our Guiding Shepherd, our Concerned Confidant. When you express loving praise to Hashem, Hashem's love for you is more vividly revealed.

I-I: Once we have deeply internalized the 'I-you' level of prayer, we can shift into the 'I-I' paradigm. In miniature, we play out this transition in our liturgy each day. In the *Pesukei d'Zimra* / verses of song we bring our loving praises of the Source of Life to a crescendo. We then recognize Hashem's unity in the Shema. Even deeper, when we first step into the Shemoneh Esrei and we utter, "Hashem, open my mouth..." we are essentially saying, 'Let my mouth be an instrument at Your disposal. I am at Your service; what would You have me say?' We ultimately want Hashem's own words to emanate from our lips, as if the *Shechina* / Divine Presence is praying through us (*Likutei Yekarim*, 1b. *Avodas Yisrael*, Metzorah).

We realize at this point that Tefilah is not meant to benefit the ego, the separate self. Rather, it is meant to benefit and amplify, as it were, the Divine Presence in the world. Thus, Tefilah is a process of the small 'i' becoming present and unified with the Divine 'I.' Ultimately, Tefilah reveals our individual ego as a distinct personal expression of Hashem's Divine Oneness.

In this way, when we use Tefilah to reveal our connection and unity with Hashem, beseeching the Creator for intercession is actually beseeching that Hashem's desire be fulfilled *through* us. Prayer thus opens us up to wanting what Hashem wants for and from us.

In fact, instead of seeing yourself as standing before Hashem in supplication, you can visualize yourself as being seen *by* Hashem. Although our conventional view of Davening may be to look outside ourselves towards Hashem and ask for assistance, a deeper level of Davening is a mode of affirmation and a process of becoming aware, again and again, of how we are an integral part of the Whole, which is Hashem.

Then, the objectives of the supplications in Shemoneh Esrei are seen to be already fulfilled in the encounter itself. The underlying answer to every prayer is to be one with Hashem. Tefilah reveals that this is our innermost desire — to be at one with the One — and also that the innermost desire of Hashem, however we are to understand this, is to be at one with us.

Three Levels within Torah

Although Torah is in general an I-I paradigm, there are also three levels within Torah: I-It, I-you and I-I.

I-it: In this level, Hashem is the giver of Torah, revealing to us what we need to do and not do. There is an absolute divide, and we may hear the Torah's voice as harsh, with demands and commands forced upon us from Above. From this perspective, we study Torah as an obligation, and in order not to fall into ignorance. We comply with what we learn and serve Hashem in *Yirah* / fear or awe, at a distance. Hashem is thus apprehended as an 'It.'

I-you: In this level, Hashem is recognized as our loving Parent who gives us the Torah as a gift. Study brings joy, as through the Torah we get to 'know' Hashem more 'personally,' as it were. We lovingly cleave to Hashem through learning and living the Torah. The words of Torah "taste sweet like honey," and we naturally want more and more, no matter which area of study.

When we authentically relate to Hashem in this way, our performance of Mitzvos is not primarily concerned with 'reward and punishment' or anxiety. Rather, the Mitzvos become conscious expressions of our overflowing love and appreciation for the Infinite One who has given us the gift of life. We come to see doing a mitzvah as shooting an arrow of love into the heart of the infinite sky. The arrow trails a cord that connects us and unifies us ever more intimately with the Holy One. Through this loving connection, our deeds can elevate us into harmony with the spirit of Divine will, to the extent that our desires are completely in sync with what our Beloved desires for and from us.

I-I: Through Torah study we can reach the deepest, most profound *Yichud* / unity and bond with Hashem, as the Tanya explains (*Likutei Amarim*, 5).

The Torah was fully and unequivocally given to human beings, according to human capacities and built-in limitations of intellect and understanding. This allows us to unify with the Torah in all areas of life, and to infuse our dreams, ambitions, aesthetics, instincts, intuitions, and modes of thinking, speaking and acting, with Divine wisdom.

The Torah was communicated to us along with a responsibility to collaborate in its development, to expound and even expand upon the Torah's primary ideas. We are asked to be *Mechadesh*, to use our intellectual, practical, and intuitive abilities to unveil and activate new Torah insights (*Zohar* 1, 12a. Alter Rebbe, *Hilchos Talmud Torah*, 1:4, 2:2. Tanya, *Igeres HaKodesh*, 26).

To be a *Mechadesh* / innovator is a Mitzvah according to the Zohar. But how, in our frail humanity, do we have the power and confidence to suggest 'innovations' within the realm of infinite Divine wisdom? The power to be Mechadesh in Torah comes from our soul's root in the Divine Essence, which is deeper than Torah or even spiritual attributes such as infinite wisdom. Ultimately, our individual 'I' is one with the ultimate 'I' of Anochi, the One Essential Self.

Book of Devarim

The book of *Devarim* / Deuteronomy, which we read throughout Elul, is the archetypal example of how the I-I relationship in Torah functions. This Fifth Book of the Torah introduces a new type of revelation. Up until this point, Hashem speaks to Moshe, and Moshe then relays Hashem's teaching to the people. The Book of Devarim, on the other hand, begins with the phrase, "These are the words that Moshe spoke." The words are apparently Moshe's.

But if this is so, why are these words included in Hashem's Torah?

The word *Deuteronomy* is derived from the Greek word *Deuteronomion*, "Second Law." In Hebrew, this book is similarly called *Mishneh Torah* / repetition of the Torah, as it re-tells all the major events experienced in the desert, as well as various laws that are already delineated in the previous four books. The entire book consists of one very long speech that Moshe delivers during the final 37 days of his life.

Devarim means 'words,' in this case referring specifically to the words of Moshe: "*Eileh haDevarim* / These are the words [that Moshe spoke to all of Israel on the East Bank of the Jordan.]" The earlier books of the Torah are also transcribed by Moshe, but they are written in third person, such as in the frequent phrase, "And Hashem spoke to Moshe, saying…" In this book, Moshe writes in first person, such as, "Hashem spoke to *me*, saying…"

In a sense, throughout the first four books of Torah, Moshe was not present as an individual with his own voice. Yet, in the Fifth Book, Moshe speaks "in his own words" (*Megilah*, 31b). He is finally present as an individual 'I,' even though his words are spoken with *Ruach ha-Kodesh* / self-less Holy Spirit (Tosefos, *ad loc.*).

In the Zohar, Rabbi Shimon says, "We were taught that the rebuke…in the book of Mishneh Torah, was (written by) Moshe by himself. Do you think that Moshe said even one small letter by himself? No, it was written with precision…(and the words that) came from Moshe's mouth, were from the voice which *possessed* Moshe" (*Zohar* V'eschanan, 265a). As many latter teachings describe, "The Shechinah was speaking through the throat of Moshe" (for earlier sources of this idea, see *Zohar* 3, 232a. *Medrash Rabbah,* Shemos, 3:15. *Mechilta*, Yisro, 18:19).

The Book of Devarim is therefore Divine wisdom just as in the first four books, however it is wisdom the way it is 'heard' and un-packed by Moshe in his individuality, and transmitted through his own unique voice. This book is thus a bridge between the Written Torah or 'Revelation of Sinai,' and the Oral Torah (*Zohar* 3, 261a). It is the confluence of the Revelation from Above and the creative in-sights of human beings below which are consistent with the spirit of that Revelation from Above.

Some even see Devarim as part of the Oral Torah (see *Abarbanel,* in his Introduction to Devarim). What is Oral Torah, essentially? In the language of the Maharal, it is the way the Torah appears from the perspective of the *Mekabel /* receiver. The Dubner Magid quotes the Gra (*Ohel Yaakov,* Devarim), to distinguish the modes of the four books and Devarim. He says that the first four books were said *through* Moshe; the Shechinah spoke through his mouth. In De-varim, however, Hashem said the words to Moshe on one day, and Moshe spoke those words to Bnei Yisrael on the following day. Basically, this implies that Moshe took time to assimilate the in-formation before giving it over; instead of channeling Hashem's word in the very moment of reception, it became one with Moshe's own intellect, and was then transmitted as his own teaching. In this sense, Devarim is not *Mamash /* literally Oral Torah, but rather a blend between Oral and Written, human and Divine, *Mekabel /* receiver and *Nosein /* Giver of Torah.

In any case, Moshe hearing the voice of the Shechinah speaking through his own throat is the perfect example of an 'I-I' relationship. He is one with the Divine 'I,' and yet he retains his individuality, as evidenced by his use of the term "me." He transcends and yet simultaneously includes himself; this is a sign of Essence-consciousness.

Torah Shel Baal Peh / The Oral Torah, is connected to the number 40. The Book of Devarim is transmitted at the end of the 40 years in the desert. Mishneh Torah (which is the way *Chazal* / the Sages refer to Devarim) has a numerical value of 246, which is the same value as the phrase, *Mem (40) Shanah Torah* / the Torah of 40 years.

What is the connection between Mem, 40, and the oral aspect of Torah? The first word of the Oral Torah, which is the first Mishnah in *Berachos*, begins with Mem: *M'eimosai* / from when? The Gemara (*Avodah Zarah*, 5b) writes that "until 40" (either in age, or forty years of learning) a person does not understand what his teacher truly means. In other words, only after '40' do the *Nosein* / giver and the *Mekabel* / receiver become unified. Similarly, 40 years after the Revelation at Mount Sinai, Hashem the *Nosein*, and Moshe the *Mekabel* (both words begin with a Mem), had become unified. Moshe's mind and way of thinking was then in complete alignment with the 'Mind' of Hashem.

There are two ways by which the Torah was given via Moshe. One is called מעבר /*Maavar* / passing through, when Moshe was merely a conduit and the Torah passed through him. This was like clear water passing through a colored glass; the water remained unchanged. The other is called התלבשות / *Hislabshus* / enclosing itself within, when the Torah was assimilated and housed within Moshe.

This was like water passing through a painted passageway; along the way, the water actually picked up a new color.

In both the modes of *Maavar* and *Hislabshus,* the 'I' of Moshe was not a separate I. In both, he had complete *Bitul* / selflessness. He was nonetheless a genuine 'I' with a distinct way of understanding and teaching. Moshe was in fact 'the perfect human being' (Rambam, *Pirush haMishnayos,* Sanhedrin Chapter 10): he was tall (*Shabbos,* 92a), strong, wealthy (*Nedarim* 38a), intelligent, just, devoted, and compassionate. This means he was fully an 'I,' fully Moshe, and he even stood out among other people. And yet when Hashem spoke to him as a Maavar, he was selflessly transparent like clear glass; his 'I' was eclipsed.

In the mode of Hislabshus, however, his 'I' was not fully eclipsed. Moshe was fully present throughout Devarim, even during a Revelation of Torah. By being fully Moshe, the I of Hashem became manifest through the I of Moshe. Moshe was one with the Divine 'I,' and his words were therefore revealing Hashem's Torah.

To some degree this is also true with us, as there is a spark of Moshe within all of us (*Tanya,* 42. *Kedushas Levi,* Re'eh). We only have the ability to be a Mechadesh when in a state of deep humility and self-nullification. And yet we must also maintain our transparent individual 'I-ness,' including our own unique way of thinking and our *Seichel* / intellectual understanding of reality. This is similar to the teaching that to be a Mechadesh in Torah you need *Yiras Shamayim* / awe of Hashem, as being in a state of awe indicates both a visceral awareness of Divinity and the continued maintenance of an identified self to register such an experience.

When we are in a state of deep humility and yet distinct individuality, our Torah thoughts can take on originality and freshness, and we too can be a real Mechadesh. The deepest level of unity with Torah activates the principle of, "Torah, Hashem, and Israel are One" (*Zohar* 1:24a). In this level we become instruments to reveal the Divine wisdom within the world.

During Elul, as we increase in Tzedakah, Tefilah and Torah, we work on all three modes of relationship with Hashem, with ourselves, and with other people. As we read the Book of Devarim throughout this month, we should allow the 'water' of Torah to permeate us, and we should assimilate it into every part of our 'I,' so that we can become greater and more expressive instruments of Divine Wisdom.

☾

APPENDIX 2:

REGRET OR RESET:
Which Comes First in Teshuva?

*T*HE RAMBAM DEFINES THE PROCESS OF TESHUVAH IN the following way (*Hilchos Teshuvah*, 2:2): "...The one who has 'missed the mark' must first 1) abandon his mistake... then, 2) resolve in his heart that he will not do it anymore... and finally, 3) regret the past." In other words, first there must be *Aziva* / abandoning the behavior, and only then can there be *Kabbalah* / taking responsibility for the future, and finally a completion of the process through *Charata* / sincere regret.

Rabbeinu Yonah, on the other hand, states (*Sha'arei Teshuvah*, 1:10-11) that there are two *Ikarim* / main ingredients in Teshuvah. העיקר הראשון - החרטה / The first main step is the *Charata*. Only after the prerequisite of 'regret' will the second *Ikar* be meaningful; עזיבת החטא / *Azivas haChet* / abandoning the mistaken behavior.

Since Rabbeinu Yonah's sequence is the opposite of the Rambam's, we need to look more deeply into the matter. In order to derive clear practical guidance and not merely choose what we want to hear, we need to determine what really should come first: regretting, or resetting the pattern of behavior.

The answer is that both sequences are correct, but they should be applied to two different circumstances. The question that we need to ask in order to determine which approach to use is whether the particular mistake is already a habitual pattern, or is it a one-time, uncharacteristic occurrence. If for you it is the latter (a one-time aberration), then you need Charata first. This is because if you already live the way you know you should, but you happened to slip, the bitterness of Charata will return you into the guidance of your sensitive conscience. Then you can proceed with Aziva and take responsibility for preventing further occurrences in the future, as Rabbeinu Yonah writes.

It is important to point out that there is 'Charata of the heart' and 'Charata of the mind.' For Charata to be effective, it needs to be 'Charata of the heart,' and not just an intellectual exercise. If you decide mentally that something is not good for you, this objective idea may not make any practical difference. This is because our lower behaviors and appetites are ultimately driven by what feels better. Therefore, our Teshuvah-response must employ the power of feeling. There must be a direct relationship between the mistake and the resulting feelings. If the bodymind recognizes the causal relationship between the mistake and heartfelt feelings of regret, it won't be drawn to making the behavior into a habit, and it will be more easily abandoned.

The problem is when 'missing the mark' becomes a habit or a way of life. At this point, self-destructive behavior becomes your second nature. In this predicament, Charata will not help as a first step, because it will not be fully sincere. Since the 'positive' feelings associated with the behavior are much more strongly established, you may have Charata for a moment, but you will revert to those stronger associations that reward and support such behavior. The unpleasant feeling of regret simply has no chance to push back against the already imprinted pleasant or numbed feelings connected with the habitual behavior. Your instinct will be merely to reject the temporary irritation of Charata. You are, in such a case, no longer living within the guidance of a sensitive conscience, in which irritation can reorient you. For Teshuvah to be effective in this circumstance, another approach must be taken.

As taught by the Meor Einayim (*Vayeitze*), the 613 Mitzvos are inscribed, as it were, on our soul. When you guard the prohibition of stealing, for example, the inscription remains intact and clearly legible: *Lo Signov* / Do not steal. These words are like an inner command, influencing your consciousness, identity, and behavior. Naturally, you will not steal as stealing is simply not part of your identity. However, the moment you slip and steal, *Chas veShalom*, the word *Lo* becomes separated from *Signov*, and your inner command becomes, *Signov* / steal! If the misdeed is repeated and a habit is created, the inscription is deepened, and stealing may even begin to appear to you as a Mitzvah. It thus becomes your new identity.

In this circumstance, you must first engage *Aziva*, abandoning the negative action and corresponding false identity immediately and completely. Pausing to engage in regret will only provide a stimulus to return to the momentary comfort of the habit. Only once you drop the behavior can you honestly take responsibility for your future behavior, and only then will your feelings of regret have leverage over your prior conditioning. You need to pull yourself up to a higher vantage point in order to get a comprehensive view of your situation and reconfigure your inner guidance system. When your identity and feelings are re-wired to harmonize with the actual Divine Mitzvah, you can then have real Charata about how you used to live, which will then serve to propel you further along the path of righteousness. This process is consistent with the Pasuk that the Rambam brings in the teaching we quoted above: כי אחרי שובי נחמתי /*Ki Achar Shuvi, Nichamti* / After I did Teshuvah, I regretted (my deeds) (*Yirmiyahu*, 31:18).

To be abundantly clear, if a person with an ingrained negative habit or addiction repeatedly applies Charata without stopping the behavior, all they are left with is a temporary feeling of negative regret about themselves. This does nothing to stop the behavior, and might actually exacerbate and reinforce the erroneous habit. Therefore, this person needs to start with 'stopping.' And the stopping should not be motivated by regret; it must be a positive, hopeful, even joyful act of stopping.

One of the best ways to positively stop a habitually negative behavior is to vividly imagine that you are a tzadik, full of love and joy and resonating internally with the Divine Mitzvos. Your greatest pleasure is in Tzedakah, Tefilah and Torah, and negative behavior is simply not part of your identity or nature. Once you are visualizing this strongly, do something to act on it. Then repeat that action, and repeat it until it becomes a new habit, supplanting the previously engrained negative pattern. It takes 40 days to transform our nature, and the 40 days from Rosh Chodesh Elul to Yom Kippur are a perfect opportunity to do so. They are, as we have mentioned, a veritable Mikvah of time in which we may immerse, purify, and transform ourselves on the deepest level.

Even if you strongly feel that you are imperfect or out of tune, your soul is still inscribed with many, many intact Mitzvos. Acknowledge and amplify your strengths and other good points will spontaneously come into alignment. You were created with a powerful propensity for Teshuvah, and there is never a reason to give up. The King of all Existence desires to be close to you; in fact, He is in the field searching for you! In this month of Divine Desire, do not hesitate to take up the Royal invitation.

Blessings for success, and for a beautiful and blessed New Year.

Other Books by the Author

RECLAIMING THE SELF
The Way of Teshuvah

Teshuvah is one of the great gifts of life. It speaks of a hope for a better today and empowers us to choose a brighter tomorrow. But what exactly is Teshuvah? How does it work? How can we undo our past and how do we deal with guilt? And what is healthy regret without eroding our self-esteem? In this fascinating and empowering book, the path for genuine transformation and a way to include all of our past in the powerful moment of the now, is explored and demonstrated.

THE MYSTERY OF KADDISH
Understanding the Mourner's Kaddish

The Mystery of Kaddish is an in-depth exploration into the Mourner's Prayer. Throughout Jewish history, there have been many rites and rituals associated with loss and mourning, yet none have prevailed quite like the Mourner's Kaddish Prayer, which has become the definitive ritual of mourning. The book explores the source of this prayer and deconstructs the meaning to better understand the grieving process and how the Kaddish prayer supports and uplifts the bereaved through their own personal journey to healing.

UPSHERNISH: The First Haircut
Exploring the Laws, Customs & Meanings
of a Boy's First Haircut

What is the meaning of Upsherin, the traditional celebration of a boy's first haircut at the age of three? Why is a boy's hair allowed to grow freely for his first three years? What is the deeper import of hair in all its lengths and varieties? What is the meaning of hair coverings? Includes a guide to conducting an Upsherin ceremony.

A BOND FOR ETERNITY
Understanding the Bris Milah

What is the Bris Milah – the covenant of circumcision? What does it represent, symbolize and signify? This book provides an in depth and sensitive review of this fundamental Mitzvah. In this little masterpiece of wisdom – profound yet accessible —the deeper meaning of this essential rite of passage and its eternal link to the Jewish people, is revealed and explored.

REINCARNATION AND JUDAISM
The Journey of the Soul

A fascinating analysis of the concept of Gilgul / Reincarnation. Dipping into the fountain of ancient wisdom and modern understanding, this book addresses and answers such basic questions as: What is reincarnation? Why does it occur? And how does it affect us personally?

INNER RHYTHMS
The Kabbalah of MUSIC

Exploring the inner dimension of sound and music, and particularly, how music permeates all aspects of life. The topics range from Deveikus/Unity and Yichudim/Unifications, to the more personal issues, such as Simcha/Happiness and Marirus/ sadness.

MEDITATION AND JUDAISM
Exploring the Jewish Meditative Paths

A comprehensive work encompassing the entire spectrum of Jewish thought, from the sages of the Talmud and the early Kabbalists to the modern philosophers and Chassidic masters. This book is both a scholarly, in-depth study of meditative practices, and a practical, easy to follow guide for any person interested in meditating the Jewish way.

TOWARD THE INFINITE

A book focusing exclusively on the Chassidic approach to meditation known as Hisbonenus. Encompassing the entire meditative experience, it takes the reader on a comprehensive and engaging journey through this unique practice. The book explores the various states of consciousness that a person encounters in the course of the meditation, beginning at a level of extreme self-awareness and concluding with a state of total non-awareness.

THIRTY – TWO GATES OF WISDOM
Awakening through Kabbalah

Kabbalah holds the secrets to a path of conscious awareness. In this compact book, 32 key concepts of Kabbalah are explored and their value in opening the gates of perception are demonstrated.

THE PURIM READER
The Holiday of Purim Explored

With a Persian name, a masquerade dress code and a woman as the heroine, Purim is certainly unusual amongst the Jewish holidays. Most people are very familiar with the costumes, Megilah and revelry, but are mystified by their significance. This book offers a glimpse into the hidden world of Purim, uncovering these mysteries and offering a deeper understanding of this unique holiday.

EIGHT LIGHTS
8 Meditations for Chanukah

What is the meaning and message of Chanukah? What is the spiritual significance of the Lights of the Menorah? What are the Lights telling us? What is the deeper dimension of the Dreidel? Rav Pinson, with his trademark deep learning and spiritual sensitivity guides us through eight meditations relating to the Lights of the Menorah, the eight days of Chanukah, and a fascinating exploration of the symbolism and structure of the Dreidel. Includes a detailed how-to guide for lighting the Chanukah Menorah.

THE IYYUN HAGADAH
An Introduction to the Haggadah

In this beautifully written introduction to Passover and the Haggadah, we are guided through the major themes of Passover and the Seder night. This slim text, addresses the important questions, such as: What is the big deal of Chametz? What are we trying to achieve through conducting a Seder? What's with all that stuff on the Seder Plate? And most importantly, how is this all related to freedom?

PASSPORT TO KABBALAH
A Journey of Inner Transformation

Life is a journey full of ups and downs, inside-outs, and unexpected detours. There are times when we think we know exactly where we want to be headed, and other times when we are so lost we don't even know where we are. This slim book provides readers with a passport of sorts to help them through any obstacles along their path of self-refinement, reflection, and self-transformation.

THE FOUR SPECIES
The Symbolism of the Lulav & Esrog

The Four Species have inspired countless commentaries and traditions and intrigued scholars and mystics alike. In this little masterpiece of wisdom both profound and practical - the deep symbolic roots and nature of the Four Species are explored. The Na'anuim, or ritual of the Lulav movement, is meticulously detailed and Kavanos,, are offered for use with the practice. Includes an illustrated guide to the Lulav Movements.

THE BOOK OF LIFE AFTER LIFE

What is a soul? What happens to us after we physically die?

What is consciousness, and can it survive without a physical brain?

Can we remember our past lives?

Do near-death experiences prove immortality?

What is Gan Eden? Resurrection?

Exploring the possibility of surviving death, the near-death experience and a glimpse into what awaits us after this life.

(This book is an updated and expanded version of the book; Jewish Wisdom of the Afterlife)

THE GARDEN OF PARADOX:
The Essence of Non - Dual Kabbalah

This book is a Primer on the Essential Philosophy of Kabbalah presented as a series of 3 conversations, revealing the mysteries of Creator, Creation and Consciousness. With three representational students, embodying respectively, the philosopher, the activist and the mystic, the book, tackles the larger questions of life. Who is G-d? Who am I? Why do I exist? What is my purpose in this life? Written in clear and concise prose, the text, gently guides the reader towards making sense of life's paradoxes and living meaningfully.

BREATHING & QUIETING THE MIND

Achieving a sense of self-mastery and inner freedom demands that we gain a measure of hegemony over our thoughts. We learn to choose out thoughts so that we are not at the mercy of whatever belches up to the mind. Through quieting the mind and conscious breathing we can slow the onrush of anxious, scattered thinking and come to a deeper awareness of the interconnectedness of all of life.

Source texts are included in translation, with how-to-guides for the various practices.

VISUALIZATION AND IMAGERY:
Harnessing the Power of our Mind's Eye

We assume that what we see with our eyes is absolute. Yet, beyond our ability to choose what we see, we have the ability to choose how we see. This directly translates into how we experience life. In a world saturated with visual imagery, our senses are continuously assaulted with Kelipa/empty/fantasy imagery that we would not necessarily choose. These images can negatively affect our relationship with ourselves, with the world around us, and with the Divine. This volume seeks to show us how we can alter that which we observe through harnessing the power of our mind's eye, the inner sanctum of our imagination. We thus create a new way to see and experience the world. This book teaches us how to utilize visualization and imagery as a way to develop our spiritual sensitivity and higher intuition, and ultimately achieve Deveikus/Unity with Hashem.

SOUND AND VIBRATION:
Tuning into the Echoes of Creation

Through our perception of sound and vibration we internalize the world around us. What we hear, and how we process that hearing, has a profound impact on how we experience life. What we hear can empower us or harm us. A defining human capacity is to harness the power sound -- through speech, dialogue, and song, and through listening to others. Hearing is primary dimension of our existence. In fact, as a fetus our ears were the first fully operating sensory organs to develop.

This book will guide you in methods of utilizing the power of sound and vibration to heal and maintain mental, emotional and spiritual health, to fine-tune your Midos and even to guide you into deeper levels of Deveikus / conscious unity with Hashem. The vibratory patterns of the Aleph-Beis are particularly useful portals into our deeper conscious selves. Through chanting and deep listening, we can use the letters and sounds to shift our very mindset, to induce us into a state of presence and spiritual elevation.

THE POWER OF CHOICE:
A Practical Guide to Conscious Living

It is the essential premise of this book that we hold the key to unlock many of the gates that seem closed to us and keep us from living our fullest life. That key we all hold is the power to choose. The Power of Choice is the primary tool that we have at our disposal to impact the world and effect change within our own lives. We often give up this power to outside forces such as the market, media, politicians or peer pressure; or to internal forces that often function beyond our conscious control such as ego, anger, lust, greed or jealousy. Making conscious, compassionate and creative decisions is the cornerstone of living a mature and meaningful life.

MYSTIC TALES FROM THE EMEK HAMELECH

Mystic Tales of the Emek HaMelech, is a wondrous and inspiring collection of stories culled from the Emek HaMelech. Emek HaMelech, from which these stories have been taken, (as well as its author) is a bit of a mystery. But like all good mysteries, it is one worth investigating. In this spirit the present volume is being offered to the general public in the merit and memory of its saintly author, as well as in the hopes of introducing a vital voice of deeper Torah teaching and tradition to a contemporary English speaking audience

INNER WORLDS OF JEWISH PRAYER
A Guide to Develop and Deepen the Prayer Experience

While much attention has been paid to the poetry, history, theology and contextual meaning of the prayers, the intention of this work is to provide a guide to finding meaning and effecting transformation through the prayer experience itself.

Explore: *What happens when we pray? *How do we enter the mind-state of prayer? *Learning to incorporate the body into the prayers. *Discover techniques to enhance and deepen prayer and make it a transformative experience.

This empowering and inspiring text, demonstrates how through proper mindset, preparation and dedication, the experience of prayer can be deeply transformative and ultimately, life-altering.

WRAPPED IN MAJESTY
Tefillin - Exploring the Mystery

Tefillin, the black boxes and leather straps that are worn during prayer, are curiously powerful and mysterious. Within the inky black boxes lie untold secrets. In this profound, passionate and thought-provoking text, the multi-dimensional perspectives of Tefillin are explored and revealed. Magically weaving together all levels of Torah including the Peshat (literal observation), to Remez (allegorical), to Derush, (homiletic), to Sod (hidden) into one beautiful tapestry. Inspirational and instructive, Wrapped in Majesty: Tefillin, will make putting on the Tefillin more meaningful and inspiring.

SECRETS OF THE MIKVAH:
Waters of Transformation

A Mikvah is a pool of water used for the purpose of ritual immersion; a place where one moves from a state of Tumah; impurity, blockage and death—to a place of Teharah; purity, fluidity and life.

In SECRETS OF THE MIKVAH, Rav Pinson delves into the transformative powers of the Mikvah with his trademark all-encompassing perspective that ranges from the literal, Pshat observation and Halachic implications of the texts, to the allegorical, the philosophical, and finally, to the deep secrets of the Mikvah as revealed by Kabbalah and Chassidus.

This insightful and inspirational text demonstrates how immersion in a Mikvah can be a transformative and life-altering practice, and includes various Kavanos—deep intentions—for all people, through various stages of life, that empower and enrich the immersion experience.

THE SPIRAL OF TIME:
A 12 Part Series on the Months of the Year.
The following titles from the series are now available!

THE SPIRAL OF TIME:
Unraveling the Yearly Cycle

Many centuries ago, the Sages of Israel were the foremost authority in the fields of both astronomical calculation and astrological wisdom, including the deeper interpretations of the cycles and seasons. Over time, this wisdom became hidden within the esoteric teachings of the Torah, and as a result was known only to students and scholars of the deepest depths of the tradition. More recently, the great teachers, from R. Yitzchak Luria (the Arizal) to the Baal Shem Tov, taught that as the world approaches the Era of Redemption, it is a Mitzvah / spiritual obligation to broadly reveal this wisdom.

"The Spiral of Time" is volume 1 is a series of 12 books, and serves as an introductory book to the basic concepts and nature of the Hebrew calendar and explores the special day of Rosh Chodesh.

THE MONTH OF SHEVAT:
ELEVATING EATING
& The Holiday of Tu b'Shevat

Each month of the year radiates with a distinct Divine energy and thus unique opportunities for growth, *Tikkun* and illumination. According to the deeper teachings of the Torah, all of these distinct qualities, opportunities and natural phenomena correspond to a certain data set. That is, the nature of each month is elucidated by a specific letter of the Aleph Beis, a tribe, verse, human sense, and so forth. The month of Shevat is particularly connected to food and our relationship to bodily intake. During this month we celebrate Tu b'Shevat, the New Year of the Tree, and aspire to create a proper and physically/emotionally/spiritually healthy relationship with food.

THE MONTH OF IYYAR: EVOLVING THE SELF

& The Holiday of LAG B'OMER

The month of IYYAR is the second month of the spring, a month that connects the Redemption from Egypt in Nissan with the Revelation of Torah in Sivan. The Chai/ Eighteenth day of the Month is the day we celebrate the Rashbi (Rabbi Shimon Bar Yochai) and the revealing of the hidden aspects of the Torah. This is the 'Holiday' of Lag b'Omer. The book explores the unique quality of this special month, a month that has a Mitzvah of counting the Omer every day. In addition, the book explores the roots and significance of the mystical 'holiday' of Lag b'Omer. Including the customs & Practices of Lag b'Omer, such as, bonfires, bows & arrows, parades, Upsherin, and more.

THE MONTHS OF TAMUZ AND AV:

Embracing Brokenness –
17th of Tamuz, Tisha B'Av, & Tu B'Av

Each month and season of the year, radiates with distinct Divine qualities and unique opportunities for growth and Tikkun.

The summer month of Tamuz and Av contain the longest and hottest days of the year. The raised temperature is indicative of a corresponding spiritual heat, a time of harsher judgement and potential destruction, such as the destructions of the first and second Beis HaMikdash, which began on the 17th of Tamuz and culminated on the 9th and 10th of Av.

A few days later, on Tu b'Av, the darkness is transformed and reveals the greatest light and possibility for new life. During these summer months of Tamuz and Av we embrace our brokenness so that we can heal and transform darkness into light.

THE MONTH OF TEVES:
Refining Relationships, Elevating the Body

The quality of Teves is generally harsh—much like its counterpart Tamuz in the summer, thus the tendency for many is to hunker down, retract, curl up and wait for the month to pass by, only to reemerge when the harshness has dissipated. Think for a moment about the 'easier' months of the year, which, like gentle waves in the ocean, carry us where we want to go. We can ride these energies easily and they can propel us forward effortlessly, we just need to go with the overall flow, so to speak. The harsher months, on the other hand, can be compared to the more powerful waves that emanate from the belly of the ocean, which come forcefully crashing down and can easily drown a person before they even realize what has happened. However, those who want to utilize the momentum of the powerful energy that is available during such times can, with caution and creativity, harness these intense waves and ride them higher and farther than other, more gentle circumstances may allow. However, harnessing the power of Tohu, the raw energy of the body, does in fact need to be approached with great care and attention.

Printed in the USA
CPSIA information can be obtained
at www.ICGtesting.com
LVHW050515130224
771375LV00002B/148